The Fourth Year of
THE
Nixon Watch

The Fourth Year of
THE
Nixon Watch

BY

JOHN OSBORNE

Cartoons by PAUL CONRAD

LIVERIGHT

NEW YORK

LIVERIGHT

This book consists of articles that appeared in
The New Republic between January 1972 and
January 1973. The title is derived from "The
Nixon Watch," the standing head under which
John Osborne reports the Presidency for that
magazine. Apart from some changes of tense for
present clarity, the correction of typographical and
similar errors, and the addition of updating ad-
denda at the ends of a few chapters, the originals
have not been altered for this publication. All
articles are reprinted by permission of the
publisher.

International Standard Book Number: 0-87140-560-1
Library of Congress Catalog Card Number: 72-97490

Manufactured in the United States of America

CONTENTS

Shooting at Henry

The worst possible judge of the need for secrecy in government and of the ethics of officials who break the rules of secrecy is a working reporter such as myself. I do what I can to penetrate the official fog and I'd welcome a lot more collaboration in that endeavor than I get at the Nixon White House. It is with diffidence, therefore, that I state at the outset of this note on a recent breach of government secrecy that in my opinion the official who must have been responsible for the breach is a rat who should be dug out of his hole and fired.

The occasion for this observation is the theft from classified government files of documents that were given to columnist Jack Anderson in early December, 1971, and have been publicized by him in fragments and in text since. "Theft" is the proper word, although the responsible official looted his own files and gave facsimiles to Anderson. Jack Anderson inherited the "Washington Merry-Go-Round" newspaper column when its founder and his employer, Drew Pearson, died in 1969. Pearson was and Anderson is a master seeker and purveyor of secrets. Conducted as it is in the Anderson column, the traffic in secrets is a business that makes the columnist the instrument of sources who may be trying to use him for the noblest or the most vicious ends. My infrequent reading of "Merry-Go-Round" indicates to me that Anderson does his best to conduct it in a decent way. He appears to be more careful than Pearson was to deny the column and its outlets in some 700 newspapers to self-servers and back-stabbers. It is believable that Anderson believed, as he says he did, that the initial source of the documents in question made them available because he was convinced that the Nixon policy toward India and Pakistan was disastrously mistaken and ought to be exposed and discredited. It is also believable that Jack Anderson was had. The difficulty with the explanation that he says he accepted is that the policy was already known and discredited. Another columnist, Joseph Kraft, presented a more credible explanation of the original act of disclosure when he wrote that "most of the evidence suggests that the true cause is a vulgar bureaucratic row aimed at getting the President's chief assistant for national security affairs, Henry Kissinger."

Only five of the many documents that Anderson says he garnered in his December haul and later are alluded to here. Four of them are official and verbatim accounts of meetings of the Washington Special Action Group, the action arm of the National Security Council, on December 3, 4 and 6. The fifth document is the paraphrased text of a cable that former Republican Senator Kenneth Keating, the US ambassador in New Delhi, sent the State Department on December 8. I deduce from Anderson's cautious account of how he obtained the documents that the WSAG texts came from a single source who first offered him a dozen or so classified items and subsequently, under pressure from the columnist, let him take his pick from "a whole massive file of documents." Anderson says that the stuff came from "plural" sources and implies that their rank is such that public identification of them would embarrass the Nixon administration. The nature and variety of the documents on which Anderson has drawn in successive columns indicate that this is true of the total haul. The WSAG texts are special. Their content suggests to me, as it did to Joe Kraft, that the official who gave them to Anderson was shooting at Henry Kissinger and only incidentally, if at all, at the Indo-

Pakistan and perhaps other policies with which Kissinger is associated. It is this official whom I take to be a high-ranking rat.

Kissinger brought the publication of three of the four WSAG texts, and extensive printed quotations from the fourth, upon himself with his remark that previous references to him in Anderson columns were "out of context." Anderson, angered, gave the texts to *The Washington Post, The New York Times* and several other newspapers in order to prove that his Kissinger references were accurate understatements. The texts are fascinating documents. They illumine a part of the Nixon-Kissinger policy operation as it has never before been exposed. But it is important to distinguish between the parts of the policy process that the WSAG texts do and do not illumine. They do not, as one commentator thought they did, show how "the decisional process" actually works. The Special Action Group deals with policy after it has been laid down. Kissinger's job when he functions as WSAG chairman is to see that the military services, State, Defense, CIA and other agencies involved in foreign policy understand exactly what the President has decided and implement the decided policy exactly as he wants it to be implemented. The Anderson texts show that Kissinger performs this task with a certitude, an arrogance, a display of proxied presidential authority that smothers any tendency toward dissent that there may be in the WSAG forum. A reader may gather from the published texts that Kissinger dominates subordinate NSC bodies where preliminary policy options are discussed in the same way with the same effect. But the WSAG texts do not prove that this is the case. They make it difficult but not impossible to believe, as I have been told at the White House and elsewhere for three years, that Kissinger in these formative sessions and in the course of directing preliminary policy studies for the NSC and for the President not only welcomes but demands a variety of views and passes them to the President without distortion or dilution.

The texts show beyond doubt what no intelligent reader of an adequate newspaper could have doubted by the time Anderson's columns appeared and the Anderson texts were published. Nobody had to be told by then that the Nixon policy of supporting Pakistan and opposing India in their December conflict was instituted and pursued with ferocious intensity. A widely quoted passage in one of the WSAG texts has Kissinger saying, "I am getting hell every half hour from the President that we are not being tough enough on India. He does not believe we are carrying out his wishes. He wants to tilt in favor of Pakistan. He feels everything we do comes out otherwise." It was said in Kissinger's behalf that this was just a typical piece of humorous Kissinger hyperbole. The remark was nothing of the kind: on the day Kissinger made it, Nixon's press secretary was saying in Florida that the President was in frequent touch with Kissinger by telephone, telling him what to do about convening the UN Security Council to put the heat on India. Another passage, in the report of a Defense observer at a WSAG meeting, has Kissinger replying as follows to a timid suggestion that a statement to be presented to the UN Security Council take equal note of Indian and Pakistanian bellicosity: "The President says either the bureaucracy should put out the right statement on this, or the White House will do it." Only two passages in the texts add anything to general and prior knowledge of the policy and of the biases that conditioned it. One of these passages, obscene when the President's refusal since March of 1971 to let anyone in the administration say a word in denunciation of the Pakistan army's atrocities in East Bengal is considered, has Kissinger wondering whether propaganda capital could be made of the plight of the threatened Bihari minority after the Indians won. The other passage, not in itself surprising, has Kissinger asking whether US arms might be slipped to West Pakistan from third countries, in violation of the belated US embargo, and suggesting that Nixon might want to go even further in defense of West Pakistan if it was invaded by India.

The leaked texts give the lie to the assertions by Kissinger and others, made in the President's behalf and at his direction, that the published impression that the US was "anti-India" was "totally inaccurate." But the administration lie was never an effective lie. Events in the subcontinent, the President's own statements, the statements and actions of Kissinger and other Nixon subordinates disproved the administration claim of "absolute neutrality" well before the WSAG texts were published. A week before they appeared, for example, an editorial comment adding up the evidence and consequences of Nixon bias toward the Yahya regime in Pakistan was derived from previously published reports and printed in

The New Republic's issue of January 1–8. A quotation from Ambassador Keating's December 8 cable, all but calling the administration version a lie, appeared in *The Washington Post* on December 19. So we come back to the conclusion that somebody was shooting at Henry.

Henry will survive.

January 22, 1972

———

Eleven months later White House officials refused to say that Anderson's source or sources had or had not been identified.

For Future Reference

These notes on the President's secret effort to negotiate a settlement of the Indochina war set forth some points that it may be well to have in mind when the glow of initial surprise and approval wears off and a fuller record of the Nixon policy and performance is known.

All that is known at this writing is what the President and his agile emissary, Henry Kissinger, chose to tell in January. The first reactions of the Hanoi government and of its delegation at the Paris peace talks, which turn out to have been little more than propaganda-cover for the real negotiations, served to confirm the accuracy but not the adequacy of the Nixon-Kissinger accounts. Kissinger said that the story he told at two White House briefings and at a public press conference was not complete. At the press conference, when he identified himself as the "White House official" who had given the background briefings, he refused to give any account of the first six of his 12 secret meetings with the North Vietnamese in Paris on the ground that they were "not relevant to our present concerns." In denouncing Nixon and Kissinger for divulging "the contents of the private meetings," and in stating North Vietnam's objections to what the President called his and the Saigon government's latest "proposal for a negotiated settlement of the Indochina conflict," the Hanoi government and its Paris delegation struck precisely the attitudes that the President and Kissinger said they had encountered at the secret meetings and in other dealings with Hanoi and the National Liberation Front. But it was evident from the reactions to the President's disclosure that such issues as the postwar American presence in Southeast Asia were of more importance to Hanoi and the NLF than Kissinger said he had found them to be at the secret meetings and that the nuances of Communist resistance to the evolving US positions were more substantial than he indicated.

At one of the briefings that preceded a televised speech by the President, it was said that Mr. Nixon was blowing the biggest secret of his administration "in order to force a negotiation and to bring about a response" from Hanoi. Kissinger, talking for the record the next day and obviously enjoying the attendant glory, relegated that explanation to its proper level and implied all there is to say about the primary reason for the disclosure when he said that the decision to make it was reached in late December, after it was evident that nothing was going to come of the secret negotiations before the 1972 session of Congress convened. "Composing domestic disharmony" over the continued war and averting a repetition of last year's debate with Democratic senators who were accusing the President of refusing to respond in a meaningful way to Hanoi's bargaining points were the reasons that Kissinger put first. He could hardly have been expected to say and didn't need to say that quieting domestic dissent in this election year and discombobulating most of the prospective Democratic opponents for the presidency was Mr. Nixon's principal purpose. Three other reasons mentioned by Kissinger amounted to one quite valid but admittedly secondary reason. It was that the differences between the President's public terms and his secret terms for ending the war put him at the mercy of Hanoi propagandists and their American dupes, encouraged continued criticism of his known policy and posture at home, and thereby encouraged the Hanoi leadership to believe that if it held out long enough the President would be compelled by domestic pressure to meet the Communist terms. Kissinger's statement that the decision to blow the great secret was reached in December raised an interesting though minor question about the timing of the disclosure. The effect of delaying it until January 25 was to obscure the news of two horrendous budget deficits in the current and next fiscal years and to black out, at

"I'm asking you to put aside partisan politics this election year!"

least temporarily, further dissection of the Nixon role in the India-Pakistan conflict and its aftermath.

Kissinger and the President chose to begin their story of the secret road to the present Nixon posture with Kissinger's seventh meeting in Paris on May 31, 1971. The essence of what had passed in the previous meetings can be guessed from the known American position and the guidance that some White House reporters were getting (it can now be said) up to the time of the May meeting. The President had long since announced his readiness to accept the result of any reasonably fair and supervised election in South Vietnam, to let both the Hanoi government and the NLF participate in organizing and conducting such an election and to make any other political concession that in his view did not imperil the right of "the South Vietnamese people to determine their own future" and guarantee a Communist takeover of the Saigon government. If what I and other reporters were being told during this period was true, and I believe it was true, Kissinger's primary purpose in the meetings that occurred between August of 1969 and May of 1971 must have been to assure the Hanoi negotiators that the President was actually prepared to be more "flexible" than he felt it politically feasible to indicate in public. The Hanoi negotiators were asked to believe that all the President really demanded was a negotiated agreement which would permit the survival of a non-Communist government in Saigon—not necessarily the Thieu government—for a decent interval after an agreement was sealed. It was not enough; Kissinger was not believed and if he had been it still would not have been enough to satisfy Hanoi.

At the May 31 meeting, Kissinger offered for the first time to set a date for what he and the President regarded as complete withdrawal of American military forces from South Vietnam, "without any assurance of withdrawal by the other side," if Hanoi and the NLF would agree to a cease-fire throughout Indochina and promise to begin the release of American military and all other prisoners when the cease-fire took effect. According to Kissinger, the North Vietnamese responded that "any proposal that did not include the political element could not even be negotiated." At and during the period of subsequent meetings in June, July and August, the NLF published a seven-point proposal combining political and military "elements," the North Vietnamese produced a basically similar nine-point secret proposal, and Kissinger submitted a revised Nixon proposal that also combined political and military issues. In June, again according to Kissinger, "we accepted the nine (Hanoi) points as a basis for negotiation," thus doing what the President was accused in Hanoi and at home of refusing to do. In August, Kissinger set a dated deadline for completing American military withdrawal on August 1, 1972, *if* an overall agreement in principle to stop the fighting in all of Indochina and begin the release of prisoners was signed by or on November 1 of 1971. At the last secret meeting on September 13, Nixon authorized Kissinger to shorten the interval between agreement and final withdrawal from nine to six months. On October 11, Nixon had Kissinger transmit but not convey in person Saigon President Thieu's offer to resign with his vice president a month before an agreed election under the auspices and supervision of an "independent" electoral commission whose makeup would be subject to further negotiation. Hanoi first agreed to and then, on November 17, cancelled a 13th secret meeting to discuss the last Nixon proposal. It was substantially similar to the eight-point proposal that Mr. Nixon announced on January 25.

The terms of the announcement elided an important element of this proposal. It was a proposal for not one but two agreements, first "in principle" to the eight Nixon points and later, at any time of Hanoi's choosing, a final agreement to be negotiated in detail. A cease-fire throughout Indochina and the release of prisoners would begin when the first agreement was signed and, along with American military withdrawal from South Vietnam, the release of prisoners would be completed within six months. The proposed election would occur within six months after the second agreement was signed, enabling Hanoi to postpone the election until all American troops were gone. A requirement for mutual withdrawal from Laos and Cambodia was implied but not stipulated in the Nixon draft. Hanoi's refusal to discuss the offered terms left the President in a position to say that it "must recognize the important difference between settlement and surrender." He implied but didn't say that his American critics and potential opponents must recognize the same difference. He's right.

February 5, 1972

Vietnam Scorecard

After the President broke the pledge of secrecy that he and Henry Kissinger had given the Hanoi government and extracted from it, and disclosed that hidden peace negotiations had been going on since August of 1969, Kissinger said with a sardonic show of courtesy that he and Mr. Nixon would "have no objection" if the North Vietnamese published the nine-point proposal for a settlement of the Indochina war that they presented in Paris last June 26. The Hanoi delegation in Paris released the proposal on January 31, along with a remarkably mild statement of the North Vietnamese position, the text of an eight-point US proposal submitted on October 11, and the texts of five messages that had passed between the two governments. The US versions of these and a few other documents were then released in Washington. In conjunction with the President's speech of January 25, the text of a revised eight-point proposal that he then announced and the transcripts of three explanatory sessions that Kissinger had with Washington correspondents, this material made the record as complete as it probably will be for a long time. But, to repeat a point made in my previous report, it is important to realize that the record is far from complete. We have the barest outline of the voluminous reports that Kissinger made to the President after each of his 12 secret sessions with the Hanoi negotiators in Paris.

Kissinger said in Washington that "we do not want to be forced to prove" that the Hanoi negotiators demanded not only that the US withdraw all support of the Saigon government but that it act "to change the government directly." He also said, rather ironically in the circumstances, that he and the President wish "to protect the confidentiality of these negotiations to the maximum" and to avoid "a debate with the North Vietnamese that would force any more of this record into the open."

The suggestion here is not that Nixon and Kissinger have deceived us. With one exception to be noted, the statement and texts released by Hanoi are consistent with and largely verify everything of substance that the President and Kissinger chose to say about the secret negotiations, the progress in them toward reducing seven of the nine differences defined by the Hanoi proposal of June 26 "to manageable proportions," and the nature and gravity of the two fundamental differences that remain as far from resolution as they were when Mr. Nixon initiated the secret effort in 1969. These differences are over the extent and terms of US military withdrawal from Indochina and how far the US is willing to go in opening the way to Communist control of South Vietnam. Hanoi's press spokesman in Paris said that the differences are "fundamental, like night and day," and Kissinger agreed in effect that they are. The point of stressing the incomplete record is that the true extent of past and possible "give" on each side, and therefore the chances of ending the war by negotiation, cannot be appraised with confidence so long as so much of the secret record is secret. At the moment, and in part because the President decided to make his disclosure, both sides have lost the freedom of maneuver and concession that Kissinger had in mind when he said: "The great advantage of secret negotiations is that you can leapfrog public positions without the turmoil that any change in positions brings about internationally and domestically in some of the countries concerned."

The President's one demonstrable departure from truth had to do with the cancellation of the 13th secret meeting that both sides had agreed to hold in Paris on November 20. Nixon said in his January 25 speech that "they called off that meeting" and Kissinger said, "they turned it down." They didn't; Nixon and Kissinger

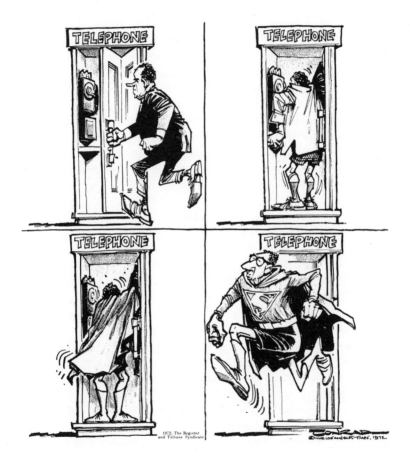

did. It's a small point, but it's one that Hanoi made a good deal of and that domestic carpers will hardly neglect. Also, the facts add to understanding of the negotiations and the tactical calculations that guided Nixon and Kissinger. The two negotiators who dealt with Kissinger in Paris were Le Duc Tho, a member of the Hanoi Politburo who came to Paris for six of the 12 meetings, and Minister Xuan Thuy, a diplomat who heads the North Vietnamese delegation at the public talks. Nixon and Kissinger proposed on October 11 that Kissinger meet again in Paris "with Mr. Le Duc Tho or some other appropriate official from Hanoi, together with Minister Xuan Thuy." Hanoi agreed October 25 to a 13th meeting but changed the date to November 20 because Tho was "busy with some work in Hanoi" and Thuy was "under medical treatment." The US agreed to the change of date on November 3, noting that it undertook and expected Hanoi to undertake to preserve secrecy. Hanoi sent word November 17 that Tho was "suddenly taken ill" but that Thuy remained "ready to hold a private meeting." Nixon and Kissinger replied November 19, hours before the meeting was to occur, that they regretted Tho's illness and that "under these circumstances, no point would be served by a meeting." Nixon and Kissinger added that "the US stands ready to meet with special adviser Le Duc Tho or any other representative of the North Vietnamese political leadership." Kissinger later said with brutal candor that he had discovered in five meetings with Thuy that there was no point in dealing with him alone. "It is no reflection on Minister Xuan Thuy," Kissinger said. "It is simply a fact of the power relationship in Hanoi that Le Duc Tho, being a member of the Politburo, has authority that no member of the Foreign Ministry has." This was true, no doubt. But it enabled Hanoi to say correctly on January 31 that Nixon had "distorted the fact" and thereby to minimize the impact of the further fact, asserted by Kissinger, that Hanoi had not responded since November to informal and secret US efforts to revive the 13th meeting.

The US demands initial agreement "in principle" on all of its eight points and "final agreement" upon all of them as they may be modified during a six-month period of further negotiation to follow the initial agreement. With a little-noticed sentence at the end of its nine points—"The above points form an integrated whole"—Hanoi also seems to demand a package agreement. It offers no equivalent of a simpler three-point deal that Kissinger presented last May 31 and that Hanoi immediately rejected: a guaranteed withdrawal of US military forces from South Vietnam within a specified period in return for a general cease-fire throughout Indochina and release of all military and "innocent civilian" prisoners by the time the US withdrawal is completed. Between June 26 and January 25, Nixon offered to reduce the withdrawal period from nine to seven and finally to six months. Always, however, he made the withdrawal conditional upon initial acceptance and final agreement, after the second phase of negotiation, of his entire package and stipulated that the withdrawal would not be completed until all US prisoners were released and other conditions were met. Nixon offers to begin withdrawal and the release of prisoners before an Indochina cease-fire is agreed to in detail and put into effect, but makes acceptance of the cease-fire a condition to complete withdrawal. Hanoi makes acceptance of all of its other proposals the condition for a cease-fire. Some experts believe that Kissinger is mistaken when he says a cease-fire was never in serious dispute during the secret negotiations and is not a critical issue now. I accept Kissinger's word for the issues that did and didn't seem acute during the negotiations and take the wording of Hanoi's eighth point to mean what it says: "*All* [my emphasis] the parties should achieve a cease-fire after the signing of the agreements on the above-mentioned problems."

There need be no argument over the political issue dividing the US and Hanoi. The clear wording of Hanoi's third point and the many amplifications of Hanoi spokesmen verify Nixon's and Kissinger's statements that the North Vietnamese demand that the US withdraw all support from the Saigon government, bargain out a deal that will place the National Liberation Front in secure control of South Vietnam, and relieve Hanoi and the NLF of the embarrassment of having to contest a popular election in South Vietnam. This is what the President calls surrender. This is what he refuses to do. And this is what he very well may have to do if events are to prove Kissinger correct when he says: "This war has to end some time, and some time it must end through negotiations."

February 12, 1972

I V

Packing for Peking

"I go to Peking without illusions," the President said in early February. He also goes with confidence that matters have been arranged so that there will be no surprises for him. The surprises, if any, will be for the world and for the American electorate, in the shape of some unexpected claims of substantial accomplishment. Mr. Nixon is smart enough to know that the sheen of the trip itself, the first visit of a US President to China and the astonishing reach of *this* President for normal relations with Communist China, will have lost its glitter by voting time next November unless he is able at the end of the journey and in the following months to say and show that he brought away from Peking and Hangchow and Shanghai something more than the sight of him on television at home, being greeted by Chou En-lai and Mao Tse-tung and sitting down with them to discuss the making of a different and better world. The President reflected his certainty that he will have something more to claim and show, and indicated the enormous care with which the trip has been prepared, when he said in his third annual foreign policy report that at his meetings with the Chinese "we will each know clearly where the other stands on the issues that divide us."

A sense of assurance that nothing can go wrong, that no sour notes of anything more than obvious and acknowledged differences between the two governments will be allowed to mar the adventure, was evident at the White House during the days of final preparation for the President's departure. When staff colleagues of Henry Kissinger remarked to him that everything must have been pretty well set in advance, he replied, "Of course. Why else do you think I'd be as relaxed as I am?"

He was all that relaxed because he and Chou En-lai had explored with each other every issue that the Chinese and the President intend to bring up. Nixon jarred Kissinger a bit by saying during a CBS television interview in early January that Kissinger had discussed the sensitive question of North Vietnam's American prisoners during both of his preliminary visits to Peking in July and October. Once that fact was out, it was not denied at the White House that Kissinger and Chou had gone through what amounted to a thorough rehearsal of the summit discussions. The rehearsal was necessary, in the first place, in order for each party to the visit to be certain beyond foreseeable doubt that the Peking government would not embarrass Mr. Nixon by withdrawing its invitation and that he would not embarrass the Chinese by canceling his acceptance. There was also at this stage, one may guess with reason, at least a tacit understanding between Kissinger and Chou that neither government's interests would be served if the principals—Chou, Mao and Nixon—risked confronting each other with attitudes that had not been anticipated and prepared for on each side. It doesn't follow from this that the Nixon talks need be empty farces, designed only or mainly to justify the televised spectacle to be transmitted from China to the US by instant satellite. Kissinger could prepare the way and has, more completely than he wishes to say. But only the President can confirm to Chou and Mao the Nixon attitudes that Kissinger outlined to them in advance; and only the President can appraise for himself the Chinese attitudes that Kissinger reported to him. Despite the cynicism that the elaborate preparations and the convenient timing with this spring's party primaries and the developing presidential campaign induce, I am persuaded that neither the Peking Chinese on their side nor the President on his side would have undertaken so drastic a turn from their own and their governments' past patterns of policy and behavior if there were not a serious intention to seek what Nixon last week called "a solid beginning" and a mutual quest for "common ground on which to build a more constructive relationship."

Only one substantive consequence of the visit was predicted last week by Kissinger at two of his increasingly frequent on-the-record press conferences in Washington. It was agreement upon a limited form of diplomatic communication, short of formal recognition of each government by the other but enough to demonstrate progress toward the "normalization of relations" that Nixon has been saying he wants. Finding agreed language to announce this much should be fairly simple. The difficulty foreseen at the White House before the President's journey was in finding words in which to announce and explain tangible understandings that the Peking government is unlikely to want set forth in tangible terms. Such an understanding will, if Nixon's hopes are fulfilled, have to do with the Republic of China on Taiwan and its relationship with the People's Republic on the mainland. A modest success can be claimed by the President if he, either alone or in a joint expression with the Peking government, is able to indicate at the end of the visit that the Chinese Communists go along with his proposition that "the ultimate relationship between Taiwan and the mainland" is a matter for "peaceful resolution" by the two Chinas. Much could be made by the President and his spokesmen, possibly more than actual discussions and resultant understandings warrant, of the barest indication that the Peking leadership agrees with Nixon that a negotiated settlement of the Indochina war is preferable to continued and abortive warfare. The prospect of Communist China's participation in a multinational conference aimed at neutralizing and stabilizing the whole of Indochina was discussed by Kissinger during his preliminary talks in Peking and it, too, could be the subject of intangible hints at a tangible undertanding.

A participant in a recent White House staff discussion of Nixon's China policy recalls that the official who conducted the session opened it by saying, "We know why we are going to Peking. The really interesting question is, why do the Chinese Communists want us to come? We don't know why, but we have some assumptions that suggest answers."

The first of two assumptions then stated was that the Peking leadership is deathly afraid of the Soviet Union and its nuclear power. The official said that he can imagine the Peking leaders imagining the men in the Kremlin ripping pages from their calendars at the end of each day—here the official made a ripping motion—and muttering to themselves that the Chinese have had another day to build up their nuclear arsenal for a strike at the Soviet Union. A leadership so preoccupied with fears may think it altogether possible that a day may come when the Kremlin leadership decides to obliterate China's centers of nuclear power with a preemptive strike. May it not (the official continued) be supposed that a leadership in such a state of apprehension has concluded that accommodation with the US is not only worthwhile but perhaps essential for survival? Not with any thought of protective military alliance—that is not conceivable—but worthwhile for whatever comfort an accommodation and the friendship that it connotes would give the Chinese and for whatever pause it may give the Kremlin leadership.

The second assumption thrown out for discussion was that the Chinese somehow perceive in accommodation with the US a means of preserving and increasing their ability to influence events in Asia and particularly in Southeast Asia. The official noted that with some exceptions (Korea; the brief invasion of India in the 1960s), the Chinese have been meticulous in their care to keep their military forces within their borders and to influence events beyond their borders by nonmilitary means. Witness the fact that their intervention in the Vietnam war has been limited to material aid. Just how accommodation with the US could enhance Chinese Communist influence in neighboring Asia was not made clear. Other assumptions, involving such factors as China's fear of Soviet political penetration and of a Japan in alliance with the US, didn't figure in the particular discussion. But the ones that did are consistent with the underlying Nixon-Kissinger calculation that the approach of the US toward accommodation in its fundamental interest can succeed only if the same accommodation is believed by the leaders of Communist China to be in their fundamental interest. Identifying the points where the interests of the two nations can be merged or at least reconciled is the essence of the President's task and hope during his visit to Peking.

February 19, 1972

V

Mission to China

Peking

At a ballet staged for the Nixons on the second night of their stay in China, the thought came that we of the President's press party really were in attendance upon a dream. The ballet was *The Red Detachment of Women*, the tale of a peasant's daughter who escaped the clutches of a cruel landlord and his running dogs, joined the Red Army, and fought with it and the broad revolutionary masses (who appeared to include a large proportion of beautiful women) until the victory of 1949 was won and the People's Republic was established "under the banner of Mao Tse-tung." It was a crude and simple tale, superbly presented, in which all of the enemies of the revolution were villains and all of its heroes were paragons of proletarian virtue. The landlord (suitably slain by the peasant's daughter) and his evil henchmen could, without excessive strain of the imagination, have been taken to typify Mr. Nixon's wealthy supporters and many of his other admirers at home. The brave and glowing fighters "for the freedom of all mankind," as the official synopsis of the ballet described them, could with equal ease have been supposed to represent Mr. Nixon's "campus bums" and militant segments of the Students for a Democratic Society. And there were Richard Nixon and his wife, applauding the show and, after it was over, thanking Premier Chou En-lai and Chiang ching, the small and demure and formidable wife of Chairman Mao Tse-tung, for arranging it and going with them to see it.

For the reporters who arrived on Sunday afternoon, 16 hours ahead of the President, the dream began in the wintry dusk that shrouded the way from the Peking Central Airport into the city. It was a poor time and a good time for getting to the city that Richard Nixon had been yearning and plotting to visit at least since 1967, when he wrote in a famous magazine article of the need to bring the United States and the People's Republic of China into accord. It was a poor time in the sense that we were weary, dulled by 13 hours in the air on the trip from Honolulu with brief stops at Guam and Shanghai. The doctors and advance men who counseled Mr. Nixon to break his journey across the international dateline with two nights in Honolulu and another in Guam were wise. The reporters had the same two nights in Honolulu, but the sudden leap from our Saturday to China's Sunday and the welcome at the Shanghai airport, meant by our Chinese hosts to be friendly and pleasant, but wearing because it made for useless delay, left us in a mood to be captious and disillusioned. We were both, and it was a good thing that we were.

In our fascination with our marginal share in a great adventure that could change the world, even the few old China hands among us needed to be reminded of a point that Chou En-lai has been making since last July to American enthusiasts who have interviewed him. The point is that China, feared though it has been and mightier now than it has ever been before, is still a poor country and, in the scales of world power, a weak country. Silly though the remark that follows may seem to people who know enough to distrust instant judgments, it is true that we saw the poverty and perceived the weakness during the 40 minutes of our bus ride from the airport into Peking. Over the years, I had seen deeper poverty and national weakness in other countries of Asia and some of my companions had observed far more of it, in pre-Communist China and elsewhere, than I had. But there was something in the grey pallor of the afternoon, the rows of bare trees and the bare fields and the glimpses of huddled farm buildings and of laboring men and animals along the road, that bespoke to us the poverty and weakness that Chou En-lai emphasizes when it suits his purposes.

The ride through the western sector of Peking, down the magnificent expanse of Chang an jie Avenue and past Tien an men Square, where Mao Tse-tung proclaimed the founding of the People's Republic in 1949 and where millions of Chinese come every year to celebrate the Republic's survival and success, had a similar effect in a rather odd way. This surely was not the storied Peking, the ancient city of gentle charm that countless Chinese and foreign writers depicted in the time before Mao and his Republic. This, it seemed then and has seemed in the three days since then, is a city of massive new buildings, of national glory anticipated and exalted and yet to be realized to the full, and grimly sought until it is realized. Strangest of all to an occasional traveler who has lived with the bustle and racket of Hong Kong and Taipei, amid the sound of Chinese voices raised in continuous noisy dialogue, this Peking turns out to be a quiet city. On side streets and in back alleys off the boulevards and the immense ceremonial square where people are dwarfed by the expanse, there is a deafening and puzzling quietude.

Perhaps the pervasive quiet of Peking had something to do with the notably quiet reception that Mr. Nixon and his party got on Monday morning. We reporters related it at the time to the reception we got at the temporary press center in the Palace of Nationalities, adjoining the Nationalities Hotel where we were quartered. Our reception was at once friendly and clearly intended to remind us that we were here at the invitation and as the guests of a great country and a great government. It fell to Yu Chung-ching, a tall and authoritative official of the foreign ministry, to drive the point home. Mr. Yu, who speaks English with a British accent acquired at the London School of Economics in 1966, held forth at length upon the splendid facilities provided for us: among other things, 154 chairs at 22 tables equipped with 44 microphones; 25 teleprinter and telephone channels for communication, mostly by satellite, with the United States; 10 broadcast booths at the center and a whole new building, erected from scratch, at the airport for network studios and transmission. After noting that these conveniences had been provided by the People's Republic of China at the request of White House officials, Mr. Yu said with a rolling flourish: "If the American officials wish to use the press room for press conferences or other purposes, they are requested to raise the matter with the information office of the foreign ministry and consideration will be given to the matter." Reporters accustomed to the authoritative manner of Ronald Ziegler, the President's press secretary, absorbed the lesson and silently thanked Mr. Yu.

Ziegler said afterward that the Monday welcome "was exactly what we expected." The waiting reporters more or less expected it, too, having learned (for example) that the diplomats who represent 66 governments which recognize the People's Republic had been told on Friday, after persistent and often plaintive inquiries, that they would not be permitted to attend the President's arrival. It was an eerie welcome, all the same. No casual onlookers of any nationality were admitted to the airport. In a typical and previously agreed piece of reticence, neither Chinese nor American officials would identify the Chinese greeters until they appeared, minutes before the President's jet landed and taxied up to the terminal. Just before that happened, the United States and Chinese flags were run up two flagpoles. Fifteen other poles remained naked. Premier Chou En-lai, placid and erect and unsmiling in a grey overcoat over a dark suit, marched onto the tarmac at the last moment, at the head of 17 senior officials and a separate party of 25 junior dignitaries. A People's Liberation Army honor guard, some 500 men in khaki and blue, precisely the same height and impressively drilled, and a PLA band were in place when the presidential plane door opened and the Nixons stepped onto the ramp. Mrs. Nixon's right hand rose in a short and tentative wave, then dropped. For the first time in more than three years that I have watched him leave his plane, the President kept his hands down and still. Within five minutes it was all over—the subdued greetings at the foot of the ramp, the playing of the national anthems, the march past the honor guard, and the departure in black Chinese limousines and smaller grey sedans.

Once in Peking, down Chang an jie Avenue past Tien an men Square to the compound of government guest houses where the Nixon party was put up, the only onlookers were people who had been forbidden by the police to cross or traverse the avenue. Half a million people had been summoned to the square to greet Emperor Haile Selassie of Ethiopia, a comparable throng to honor President Ceasescu of Romania. As foreign ministry functionaries

and the interpreters assigned to the American reporters kept saying, it was proper, polite and appropriate—all, they said, that the
chief of a government that didn't recognize the People's Republic
could expect and, the available American officials said, in fact did
expect. That was true enough. But an event soon to be known
confirmed an impression that I had brought to Peking from Washington. The impression was that the Peking leaders wanted this
visit and wanted the world to believe that Mr. Nixon wanted it
more than they did. "He wanted to come so we invited him,"
Chou told interviewers last summer. This version was privately
resented and quietly countered at the White House, but not so
audibly or in such a way as to irritate Chou and Mao.

The confirming event was Chairman Mao's meeting in secret on
Monday afternoon, in his yellow-roofed and modest home in a
corner of the old Forbidden City, with Mr. Nixon before the
President got down to serious talk with Premier Chou. The President knew before he left Washington that he would meet and
confer with Mao, but he indicated during his flight from Washington that he didn't count on it happening so early in the visit. The
fact that it did was supremely important to the visitor and his
hosts, because it was a signal to the people of China that the anti-
American signs which still graced the walls on Tien an men
Square no longer meant much. There was sure to be at least one
more meeting with Mao; Chou implied the certainty when he said
not long ago that the results and significance of the Nixon visit
would not be known until the President had his "final talk with
Chairman Mao."

The crowded Monday ended with Premier Chou's obligatory
dinner for the President and his party. It was a sumptuous affair in
the monumental Great Hall of the People, one of 10 huge buildings constructed in 1958 and 1959 in celebration of the Republic's 10th anniversary. President Nixon at table with Premier Chou
and officials of the People's Republic under the American and
Communist Chinese flags and in world view by way of television
was the stuff of dreams.

Hearing the PLA band play "Turkey in the Straw" and "Home
on the Range" for an American President and his wife deserved to
be but wasn't noted by Nixon as one of his historic firsts. Watch-

ing the President touch glass some 70 times with Chinese officials at the Premier's and adjoining tables was something to remember. But it was the toasts, Nixon's to Chou and Chou's to Nixon and to their respective countries, that historians will ponder.

The most to be said for Nixon's was that it was conventionally eloquent ("This is the hour. This is the day for our two peoples to rise to the heights of greatness") and that he imitated Lincoln at Gettysburg ("What we say here will not be long remembered. What we do here can change the world"). With television obviously in mind, he read his text straight through instead of pausing at intervals, as he usually does on such occasions, for translation in the host's language. Chou paused frequently for translation, and his statement had bite in it. The bite came with his recitation of the "Five Principles of Peaceful Coexistence" that he first enunciated at the Bandung Conference in 1955. When Chou spoke of the duty of nations to practice "mutual respect for sovereignty" and "noninterference in each other's internal affairs," he was talking about Taiwan, the island home of Chiang Kai-shek's Republic of China, and once more putting Nixon on notice that there cannot be normal relations with the People's Republic so long as the United States questions Communist China's claim to Taiwan. He didn't mention other contentious issues that he has said he wants to discuss with Nixon—total American military withdrawal from Asia and the nearby Pacific, for instance—and he said the visit was "a positive move" toward "the normalization of relations." It was a happy sort of evening and it boded well for the outcome of the Nixon visit.

An important question was what and how much the Peking government would tell the people of China through its controlled media. That question was answered on Tuesday, with a bang. The government's principal newspaper, *The People's Daily*, printed on its front page a big picture of Mao greeting Nixon; another of Mao and Nixon with Chou and Henry Kissinger, and a third of Chou greeting Nixon at the airport. Four more pictures on the second page, with the texts of the Chou and Nixon toasts, completed a statement to the Chinese people that this visit had the total blessing of Chairman Mao and that they should expect good and great things for the People's Republic to flow from it. Four pictures in Wednesday's paper, one of them showing Chou, the Nixons and the Chairman's wife, Chiang ching, applauding the performers of

The Red Detachment of Women, and a spate of friendly stories, continued to prove that what we are seeing here isn't a dream.

Midway in this incredible visit, the word is that Peking is quiet and that it's snowing and that Richard Nixon, taking in an exhibition of Chinese gymnastics on Wednesday night, must be a pleased and happy President. He isn't forgetting, one may be sure, that it's 1972.

March 4, 1972

———

As will be seen in the next report, I and the officials who told me to be "sure" of a second meeting with Mao were wrong.

VI

Chinese Checkers

This account of the Nixon trip to China, written in Washington after the President's return, begins with a remembered scene in the banquet hall of the Hang-chou Hotel in the resort city of Hang-chou, the capital of Chekiang Province, where Generalissimo Chiang Kai-shek was born 85 years ago. Premier Chou En-lai is seated at the President's right, Mrs. Nixon at her husband's left. Through an interpreter, also a woman, Pat Nixon and the wife of a Chinese official are talking with a show of great animation. Premier Chou and the President have fallen silent. They have the look of men who for the moment have had more than enough of each other, and no wonder. It is the last night but one of the President's seven days in China, the days that he is soon to say made up "the week that changed the world." He and Chou have been nearly 40 hours together at public dinners and entertainments and in private converse. They have just spent a cold and windy afternoon in a tour of West Lake, the glory of China and of Hang-chou, and its lovely islets set at the foot of misty mountains, smiling into cameras and feeding goldfish and acting out for the world their portrayal of old enemies learning and trying to be friends. Premier Chou, a grey little man of 72, gazes straight ahead for minutes on end. Mr. Nixon cups his chin in his right

hand and stares upward at the high ceiling. He and his host for the
evening, Chairman Nan Pinh of the Chekiang Revolutionary
Committee, have delivered their respective toasts, mercifully brief
for once. The several hundred Chinese in the huge room have
applauded the President's quotation of the saying that "heaven is
above and beneath are Hang-chou and Soochow" and have then
received in stony and puzzled quiet his added observation that
"the proud citizens of this province would say that Peking is the
head of China, but Hang-chou is the heart of China." They would
say, an embarrassed Chinese official explains to a table of reporters, that Peking is the head and heart of China. Suddenly, the
President's third public dinner of the week and his fourth in
Chou's company is over. Nixon and Chou rise and, with the others
of the official party, walk slowly up a long aisle from the head
table to the exit. American reporters are standing along the aisle
and the President introduces some of them to Chou. Near the
door, during one such pause, the President remarks that he and
the Premier have been hard at work all week and still have work
to do that night. Chou smiles dimly and with his right hand gives
the President a gentle shove toward the door, as if to say that's
right and let's get on with it. Mr. Nixon halts once more, in a
cluster of reporters, and Chou again touches his shoulder and
urges him toward and finally through the door. Walking behind
them, an American official clutches his stomach in mock dismay
and murmurs his thanks to God that only one more Chinese banquet lies between the Nixon party and the journey home.

   This observer wouldn't know how Mr. Nixon came over on this
and other public occasions to the home and worldwide television
audience, the audience that the President twice declared with evident pleasure to be the largest that had ever witnessed an event.
To a reporter tagging along with him in China, the President
seemed to be strikingly and consciously diffident throughout the
visit. He kept his hands, those famous twitching hands, under rigid
control. This was easier than usual to do, because at no point
from the arrival in Peking to the departure from Shanghai did the
Chinese authorities allow crowds to assemble in his honor and
invite the familiar Nixon salute. The interpreters and other functionaries who accompanied the press invariably said that the few
hundreds of Chinese noted along the streets traveled by the Nixon
party would have been there anyhow. Even when they were seen

to be watching the motorcades, any special interest in their improbable visitor was explicitly denied.

One could guess that the President had been forewarned and had determined not to obtrude himself upon his Chinese hosts and the Chinese scene any more than his presence demanded. The result, in any case, was that an occasion that might have been expected to elicit some new and enlightening aspects of the Nixon personality was curiously barren in this respect. His talent for the utterance of banalities was unimpaired, as he demonstrated when he remarked at the Great Wall that "you have to conclude that this is really a great wall" and called upon Secretary of State William P. Rogers and nearby reporters to agree that it was. Mrs. Nixon, industriously providing the television crews with something to do when the President was immured in private conferences, emitted a daily stream of bright inanities. In the kitchens of the Peking Hotel, where favored guests who don't rate the handsome government guest houses are lodged in funereal grandeur, she stated that the boggling piles and varieties of Chinese food laid out for her inspection looked good enough to eat. When her host at the moment, the chairman of the hotel revolutionary committee, invited her to stay for lunch and sample the food, the consternation that sated western guests in the Far East are bound to feel from time to time was evident as she begged off and promised to return for that pleasure at some later date. In the freezing cold at the Great Wall and the Ming Tombs, in the light snow that fell over the Forbidden City and its fantastic succession of ancient palaces and museums when the President visited them, Nixon appeared as usual without a hat and was dutifully trailed by the Secretary of State and ranking aides in a condition of hatless and obvious discomfort that their master chose to ignore. When he invited the American press party to pose with him for a group picture at the guest house assigned to him in Hang-chou, he turned up in the open and chilly patio where the photograph was taken with neither hat nor topcoat and for 12 petrifying minutes assured the journalists that he understood their need for hard news from his closed and secret conferences with Chinese officials and was sorry that he couldn't do much about it until a joint communique was issued in Shanghai. These incidentals intrigued the reporters and, the Hang-chou picture episode excepted, amused them. But there was something about the China adventure that made all this seem irrelevant and inconsequential. It was as if the event and the results that could follow it dwarfed the Nixons and their less impressive characteristics and invested the President with a stature that he could not attain by and for himself alone.

The secrecy that cloaked the President's and Henry Kissinger's meetings with Premier Chou En-lai and Chairman Mao Tse-tung, and Secretary Rogers' huddles with lesser officials, was soon to affect and distort the reporting and interpretation of the announced results. The few details that could be extracted from the President's press spokesman and other American officials in China and after the return to Washington did throw some light upon the proceedings, however. It turned out to be true, as had been supposed and reported, that the President and Kissinger were as surprised as everybody else was when the rarely seen or accessible Chairman Mao received them on the Monday of their arrival. At 78, often reported in recent years to be either dead or incapacitated, Mao appeared to Nixon and Kissinger during their hour with him to be in excellent health, alert, and in total command of the People's Republic. With necessary breaks for translation allowed, the half hour or so of substantive talk that the President and Kissinger had with Mao could hardly have encompassed the range of issues that the Americans wanted the press to believe it did. Nothing whatever about the substance of the talk with Mao was divulged. The only fact that emerged, other than the Chairman's appearance of bouncy health, was that Premier Chou, who on other occasions seemed to the Americans to be the paramount and controlling figure on the China scene, played the part of a humble follower and subordinate when he was in Mao's presence with them. Chou's demeanor presumably contributed to the impression, reported by Kissinger, that the Premier checked with Mao at every important stage of the secret discussions. Nixon and Kissinger had never been told when and where they would meet Mao, and they didn't know for sure until they were about to leave China that they wouldn't have a second meeting with him.

It was intimated to Kissinger during his preparatory visits in July and October that the Chinese authorities would be offended if the President traveled within China in American rather than People's Republic aircraft. Mr. Nixon's Air Force One (properly and

pompously the Spirit of '76) and a second Boeing 707 jet delivered him and his supporting party to the Peking airport. After
that, on the short flights from Peking to Hang-chou and from
Hang-chou to Shanghai, the President and his assistants traveled
in two Ilyushin 18s. The same planes transported the press party
ahead of the President, then were flown back to Peking and Hang-
chou to pick up the Nixon group. Because other Ilyushins were to
be seen at the Peking and Shanghai airports, always grounded
while the President was anywhere near, the reporters assumed that
only these particular planes and their crews had been checked out
for safety and competence, to the satisfaction of solicitous Chinese
officials. By comparison with the spacious Boeings of the presidential fleet, the Ilyushins are cramped and noisy jet-prop craft.
They could not have carried even the minimal communications
equipment that a US President requires. Presumably without
offense to the sensitive Chinese, the President's Boeing followed
the Ilyushins by 15 minutes and was parked as inconspicuously as
possible at the Hang-chou and Shanghai airports. At the Hang-
chou airport, a rather touching symbol of Chinese pride and anxiety to measure up to the logistical demands of the Nixon visit was
observed. It was a large and attractive terminal building, beside a
smaller and shabby old one, erected within 40 days by some
10,000 laborers and artisans in September and October 1971 after
it was certain that the President would be coming to Hang-chou.

In deference to Chinese sensibilities, the President and his companions relied entirely upon interpreters provided by the People's
Republic. The same young women who served in this capacity at
the public and televised appearances translated for the President
and Kissinger at the closed conferences. The confidence thus re-
posed in Chinese officialdom was not completely unalloyed, however. John Holdridge, a Kissinger assistant who speaks and understands Mandarin Chinese, sat in at all of the President's and
Kissinger's meetings with Chou. Two State Department language
specialists accompanied Rogers at his sessions. Holdridge and his
State Department colleagues, Alfred Jenkins and Roger Freeman,
kept quiet (and generally unneeded) check upon the Chinese
translation and prepared voluminous records of the proceedings
for White House and State Department files.

One may be sure that these records are far more complete and
revealing than the "complete and adequate report" provided by

the President and his spokesmen in Shanghai and Washington proved to be. The report so described by the President's press secretary, Ronald Ziegler, consisted of the joint American and Chinese communique issued in Shanghai the evening before the President left China, Henry Kissinger's cautious elaboration of the communique at a press conference in Shanghai, and the speech that Mr. Nixon delivered when he landed at Andrews Air Force Base. My purpose in the remainder of this report is to summarize the understandings of what did and didn't transpire in China that the administration wants to convey and my estimate of the Kissinger-Nixon account.

I find it believable that the President and his Chinese conferees reached no "written or unwritten agreements." The few concrete accomplishments that are claimed—moves toward expanded trade, cultural exchanges, regular diplomatic communication short of formal recognition—justify the rather exalted Nixon estimate of their importance only in the sense that they signify the beginnings of accommodation between two powers that have been isolated from each other and in a state of declared hostility to each other since the People's Republic was founded in 1949. I doubt that the opportunity given Nixon on the American side and Chou and Mao on the Chinese side to explore and test out each other's perceptions of the world and its problems, as a somewhat enchanted American adviser to the President put it after the return to Washington, is as important and as promising for the future as Mr. Nixon is said to think it is. Since Kissinger visited Peking last July, the same informant has been telling Washington reporters how fully and admirably steeped in American lore and attitudes Premier Chou En-lai is. If Mr. Nixon had to go to Peking, as he said he did, to learn in person from the Chinese leaders of "their total belief, their total dedication to their system of government," then he and his countrymen are in a sad plight. It was not anything that Nixon could have learned anew about his Chinese hosts and their purposes, or that they could have learned about him and his purposes, that gives the Nixon visit to China substantial significance. What makes it meaningful is the fact that it occurred; that the Chinese Communists were willing to receive him and that he was willing to go to them, in defiance of ingrained and powerful prejudices and preconceptions in both countries. The enchanted American adviser whom I have just quoted, rather disparagingly, was closer to reality when he said after his return to Washington that Chou and Mao are likely to have at least as much trouble with the extremist factions in their society, in the Nixon aftermath, as the President is already having with some of his disillusioned and critical conservatives.

The conservatives are principally alarmed by what they take to be the evidence in the Shanghai communique that Nixon has agreed to sell out Chiang Kai-shek and his Republic of China on Taiwan in return for a Chinese Communist undertaking to further a negotiated settlement of the Vietnam and Indochina war. There can be no doubt that the US interest in Taiwan has taken second place to the US interest in achieving a full accommodation with Communist China. But the interest in Taiwan and the commitment to defend it against mainland military aggression were in decline before Mr. Nixon went to Peking. The suspicion that the President persuaded the Peking leadership to push the Hanoi Communists toward a settlement of the war, at the Taiwan government's expense, rests only upon the semantics and omissions of the Shanghai communique. My hunch, based upon no better evidence, is that if there was a failure in Peking it was the President's failure to make any progress toward a negotiated end of the Indochina war.

March 11, 1972

———

My hunch was wrong. Although direct evidence was still lacking at the end of 1972, it seemed clear enough that the President's discussions in Peking and Moscow encouraged the Chinese Communist and Soviet governments to encourage the Hanoi government to negotiate a settlement of the Indochina war.

VII

Back Home

Just before the President went to China, he told John D. Ehrlichman, George P. Shultz and other senior assistants who stayed at home to mind the store that he expected them to have a full domestic agenda ready for him when he got back. After a few days for him to rest up from the China trip, and for the country to absorb and appreciate the extent and implications of his anticipated success in Peking, he intended to turn with a spectacular display of activity and concern to home affairs, and the job of his top assistants in his absence was to prepare the position papers and travel schedules that this shift of posture would require.

Mr. Nixon found when he returned that the job had been done, though not to his total and immediate satisfaction. The difficulty was with the alternative schedules for domestic travel that had been drafted for him in countless hours of staff committee work. Several circumstances made the task hard for the men who were trying to satisfy the President. For one thing, they discovered that the eight weeks or so that would intervene between the return from China and the period of preparation for his Moscow trip in May seemed to afford surprisingly few occasions—conventions, community affairs, park and dam dedications, and the like—that could be made to call for and justify a presidential visit. The party primaries occurring in several states and the campaigning everywhere also complicated the task. Mr. Nixon, having said that he wouldn't campaign for reelection until after he was renominated in San Diego, ordered that he not be scheduled for appearance in any state just before or just after a primary and that none of the arranged events be so blatantly political that the dullest citizen would perceive that he was doing what he had said he wouldn't do at this stage. The biggest difficulty, however, had to do with the President himself and his impassioned refusal to be committed to any position, action or public performance that he has not personally approved. Advance commitment, or the mere impression of commitment without his explicit approval, is one of the few things that drives Nixon to open and explosive anger. His senior staff has never forgotten the lesson he gave its members in early 1970 when, in flight from Washington to his California home in San Clemente, he canceled an entire itinerary prepared for him in the Midwest and along the West Coast because he had not in his opinion been consulted in sufficient detail about each of the stops. The vaguest inquiry as to whether local officials and organizations would welcome a Nixon visit is likely to stimulate premature announcements that the President is coming, and when this happens there is trouble at the White House. In the ten days after his return from China, Mr. Nixon proved to be unusually hard to please. The word on March 8 was that he still intended to take the road, but not the roads that so far had been suggested to him.

The transition from foreign summitry to home concerns was not an instant process, however. First, the day after the President's return, there were sessions with the bipartisan congressional leadership and with the Cabinet at which Mr. Nixon appeared to be at once tired, exuberant, and serenely confident that in Peking he had made an enduring place in history for himself and changed the world for the better. His hearers learned nothing more of the substance of his talks with Mao Tse-tung and Chou En-lai than the public had been told. He did say, more emphatically and clearly than Henry Kissinger and others had said, that he discussed the Vietnam war and the obstacles to ending it with Premier Chou. Beyond that, on that subject, he didn't go. His major emphasis was

"WHAT'S CHINA GOT THAT WE HAVEN'T GOT...?"

upon the importance that he attached to the meetings themselves, to the warm welcome he got from Mao, the long hours of intimate talk with Chou, and the useful perceptions of each other that he thought he and Chou acquired. He dealt with the suspicion of some of his conservative critics that he had sold out the nationalist Chinese on Taiwan, but he didn't seem to be worried about it and said that events would show beyond argument that the charge was false. The President made a point of giving Secretary of State William P. Rogers the floor, obviously to counter the impression that Rogers had played second fiddle to Henry Kissinger in China. As he was to say a few days later at a press conference, Rogers assured the Cabinet that he was wholly pleased with the China venture and with his part in it. He told a little story about the tiny metal US flag-pins that the President gave each member of his official party, with instructions to wear them in their lapels as Mr. Nixon did. It's the kind of display that Rogers doesn't normally go for, and he said he kept forgetting during the first days in Peking to put the pin in his lapel. Then he got the point, he said, the point of pride in being an American with Nixon in China that the pins signified, and after that he wore his pin every day.

The preparatory homework began to pay off in Florida, where the President retired to rest and plan the coming domestic show. A strong restatement of his dedication to his national health plan, based upon federally and privately financed commercial insurance for everybody, and of his opposition to the much more costly plan proposed by Senator Kennedy and others, was followed in Washington by a stream of domestic pronouncements. They dramatized his claims that this administration is doing more than any previous administration has done to feed hungry Americans; to give minorities a fair shake in federal and private hiring and promotion; to provide summer jobs for deprived youngsters; to simplify and reduce the classification of government documents; and to reform and supplement with federal funds the state and local financing of public schools. The procession through the White House press room of officials and presidential commission chairmen, proclaiming and amplifying these real and alleged achievements, demonstrated the matchless capacity of an incumbent President to dominate the news and, in such a year as 1972, to run hard for reelection simply by seeming to be a zealous and active President.

Two vexatious problems marred the return. One of them was

the busing issue and the President's promise, given before he went off to China, to come clean on the way in which he would prefer to restrict the power of the federal courts to require more and more school busing. The other problem was how to deal with the suspicion of White House hanky-panky in connection with anti-trust concessions made by the Justice Department to the International Telephone and Telegraph Corporation and the subsequent pledge by one of its subsidiaries, the Sheraton Hotel Corporation, to underwrite somewhere between $100,000 and $400,000 of the cost of holding the Republican convention this summer in San Diego, a short chopper hop from the Western White House.

Few if any Nixon staff operations have exceeded, in agony and magnitude, the study of alternatives and foreseeable consequences that preceded the President's choice of a course to take on busing. His opposition to busing, on the scale required by the courts, was not in question. Neither was the fact that Nixon had done more than any other individual to make busing a corrosive and essentially deceptive national issue. The question before him was whether to advocate an effort to curb the courts by constitutional amendment or by legislation—and, if the latter, by what kind of legislation. The advice offered him went heavily against amendment and for legislation, but with very little confidence in the efficacy of any conceivable legislation. The truth on the eve of his busing pronouncement was that Mr. Nixon had got himself into a most unhappy situation. Stuck with his promise to declare some choice, he was offered alternative choices which seemed likely to engender more trouble and difficulty than they could possibly remedy. Nixon had his spokesmen say he didn't want to appear to be trying to influence the outcome of the Florida primary on March 14, in which busing was a referendum issue, or to be influenced by the Florida vote. One of the cuter suggestions made to him was that he get around this difficulty by announcing his busing preference on the day of the primary.

A fact that made the ITT controversy an especially sensitive matter for the President was generally overlooked. It was that putting the Republican convention in San Diego, a city whose leading personalities didn't ask for it on their own initiative and didn't much want it, was Mr. Nixon's personal wish and project. Two Californians on his staff, former Lieutenant Governor Robert

Finch and former San Diego editor Herbert Klein, conveyed the President's desire to the San Diego mayor and others in power there last May. Finch said publicly that it would be a shame if San Diego didn't bid for the convention, and sure enough it did and the GOP national committee chose San Diego over several other cities that really wanted it. This history may have had nothing at all to do with the established facts that Peter M. Flanigan, the corporate contact man at the White House, helped get a favorable antitrust decision for ITT; that ITT's Sheraton subsidiary thereafter promised substantial help with the convention costs; and that (as Don Bacon of the Newhouse Newspapers discovered and reported last August) it had been agreed that Mr. Nixon would stay at a new Sheraton Hotel in San Diego when he flew over from San Clemente to accept renomination. What impresses me in all this, the more sinister implications aside, is the evidence that nobody at the White House, from the President down, was bright enough to foresee the embarrassment or worse that was bound to result if and when the facts came out.

March 18, 1972

VIII

Politics and Controls

On March 7, a week after the President got back from China and immersed himself in domestic affairs, he met with the group that is variously designated at the Nixon White House, in one of that staid institution's few flights into whimsy, as the Troika and the Triad. Its three members are Treasury Secretary John B. Connally, budget director George P. Shultz, and Herbert Stein, chairman of the Council of Economic Advisers. They were asked to update the President on the state of the economy and the prospects that he would be able to say with confidence next summer and fall, when he is actively running for reelection, that his promise of prosperity with "reasonable price stability" was on the way to fulfillment. Stein, who had prepared a written report for the President, said later that Mr. Nixon never embarrasses his professional economists with blunt demands for information and advice tailored to his political needs and that he had not done so in this instance. The call for assurance that the President's unprecedented effort to control and stabilize the economy would be enough of a success by campaign time to confound the Democrats and give Mr. Nixon a winning issue was only implied, but the officials at the meeting understood that this was what they were talking about. Stein said he reported that the economy was in good shape and going to be in better shape and that the price, wage and rent control system which the President installed last November, beginning Phase 2 of the stabilization process that had started in August with an absolute freeze, was working pretty well. A reporter asked Stein whether the President could judge from what he was told at the meeting that he could expect to be saying next summer and fall, with facts to support him, that the annual rate of price inflation was coming down to the promised level of between 2 and 3 percent and that the national unemployment rate was being brought down from a politically dangerous 6 percent to a defensible 5 percent. Stein answered "Yes" and handed the reporter the text of a speech in which, he indicated, he told the New York Association of Business Economists on March 9 approximately what he had told Mr. Nixon on the 7th.

In view of what Stein was telling a group of Washington reporters within 24 hours, and of other signs that a certain unease pervaded the actual White House view of the economic prospects, it was an interesting speech. In it, Stein set forth the happy vision of "more production, less unemployment and less inflation in 1972" and said that most of the respected professional forecasts project a year to be marked by "a strong, steady, but not exuberant and not inflationary expansion." He said the Council of Economic Advisers stood by its January prediction "that the unemployment rate would decline to the neighborhood of 5 percent by the year-end and that we would achieve the goal of an inflation rate not in excess of 2 to 3 percent by year-end also." Big jumps in new housing starts, manufacturers' new orders, indicated business investment, and the rate of increase of the monetary supply permitted by the Federal Reserve Board, were among the items cited from "a quite extraordinary run" of favorable statistics. Stein acknowledged that price inflation continued to be "our most difficult if not our most serious problem," but he argued that the problem was being solved and that the two agencies responsible for direct controls, the Pay Board and the Price Commission, had set and were enforcing standards that should "yield the target rate of inflation at the end of the year." Here a note of concern that was soon to be accentuated crept into the speech. Observing that "critical confrontations between the system and powerful private groups" are bound to occur, Stein said that "the administration is aware of that and (is) prepared to use its full resources to assure the continuity and success of the system."

Stein had to deal the next day, at a press conference in Washington, with the announcement of the wholesale price index for February. After adjustment to eliminate seasonal variations, it had jumped seven tenths of one percent over the January level. That doesn't seem like much to laymen, but when it's multiplied by 12 it translates into an annual inflation rate of 8.4 percent. Given that current rate, Stein was asked whether he really thinks the goal of 2 to 3 percent by the end of the year is realistic. "Oh, yes," he answered, "I don't see any problem there." But he did see a problem there and in subsequent remarks he indicated what he thinks the problem is and isn't.

It isn't, he said, the recent rise in the prices of farm products and processed foods—cattle, hogs, meats, poultry, fish—although the increase in those prices accounted for the biggest part of the total wholesale price rise. He said that the administration's farm program, with its deliberate stimulus to farm income and the policy decision not to attempt any control of prices paid to farmers, "reflects a balance of considerations." The chief consideration, which is political, was not mentioned, but it was implicit in Stein's admission that the administration has no intention of even trying to control the prices of farm products. What it does intend, he said, is to do whatever it thinks necessary and it can do to restrain the prices of industrial commodities, principally meaning manufactured products. "That seems to me," Stein said, "to be the core of the inflation problem." In the six months before the August freeze was imposed, industrial commodities prices increased at an annual rate of 5.7 percent. In the six months after August, the rate dropped to 1.4 percent and in February alone it was only four tenths of one percent. Now, Stein said, the problem is "to get that point-four down to something like point-two" and "we are going to do what we can to make it happen."

The instruments for doing whatever is done "to make it happen" are the President's Cabinet-level Cost of Living Council, the Pay Board, and the Price Commission. Mrs. Marina Whitman, the first woman appointed to the Council of Economic Advisers, said, after Stein dropped his intimations of concern and of further action, that stiffer controls than those so far sanctioned by the Cost of Living Council and imposed by the Pay Board and the Price Commission may be necessary if critical prices don't soon stop rising. Any such action on a broad and effective front would require some very delicate maneuverings and negotiations between the Cabinet Council, which determines overall stabilization policy, and the Pay Board and Price Commission, which apply the policy in specific cases and like to believe that they evolve a good deal of their own policy without White House dictation.

George Meany of AFL-CIO and the four other labor members of the Pay Board agreed to join the five management and five "public" members only after the President promised last October that its decisions would not be subject to appeal to the Cabinet Council. Meany and his brethren interpret the promise to rule out any presidential interference with the board's business, which at best entails enormous strains between the labor members and other members. The result is that the council's chairman, John Connally, and its staff director, Donald Rumsfeld, inject themselves into the board and commission affairs only with the greatest caution. Rumsfeld, a sunny sort of fellow who is adept at making difficult situations seem less difficult than they are, acknowledges that the council has caused both the board and the commission to bring some speed and order into their originally slow and disorderly procedures, and to correct some early rulings that were thought to be either impracticable or unfair, or both. But he says that it's all been done by consultation and persuasion, not by dictate, and one may assume that any serious stiffening of wage and price standards would call for much stiffer direction from the council to the board and commission than the officials acting for the President have dared to risk up to now.

It may also be assumed that stiffer direction from on high will be forthcoming if Mr. Nixon concludes that the prospects outlined to him by his Trioka-Triad on March 7 were too rosy by far and that the later indications of doubt that the stabilization program has been adequately stabilizing are justified. The single certainty in a sea of economic uncertainties is that the President isn't about to let a Nixon inflation do him out of reelection.

March 25, 1972

———

Who would have supposed, when the above was written, that the
President would early in 1973 abolish the Pay Board and Price
Commission, abandon most of the specific controls, and send
Donald Rumsfeld off to Brussels as Ambassador to NATO? I
didn't.

There Goes the Bus

The first thing to be said about Mr. Nixon's latest statements and proposals on the subject of school busing is that the busing he says he opposes—"busing for the purpose of achieving racial balance in our schools" and "massive busing to achieve racial balance"—does not exist. The busing that the President opposes and undertakes to halt has been ordered by federal agencies and by the courts for the purpose of desegregating racially segregated public schools. In its several possible meanings, none of which has ever been identified by Mr. Nixon as the one he has in mind, "racial balance" may describe any one of a variety of school and classroom conditions that officials and judges have deemed it necessary to bring about in order to accomplish desegregation. But racial balance in itself is not and never has been the purpose of federally required busing and desegregation. A Nixon official who knows that this is true, and who therefore must perceive that the President's habitual characterization of the busing issue is seriously misleading, is Elliot Richardson, the Secretary of Health, Education, and Welfare. At a White House briefing for the press on March 17, after Mr. Nixon had equated busing with racial balance four times in a 12-minute speech over national television and had submitted a busing message and two pieces of anti-busing legislation to Congress, a reporter put the following statement and ques-

tion to Secretary Richardson: "You know of no decision by a
court that has ordered busing for the purpose of achieving racial
balance. Is that correct?" With a look of acute discomfort, Richardson answered, "Yes, that is correct."

Mr. Nixon and his sensitive assistants are in no position to
claim that the point just made is a picayune and irrelevant play
upon semantics. "In short," the President said in his busing message to Congress, "this is not the simple black-white issue that
some simplistically present it as being." Indeed it isn't, and I
herewith acknowledge that I am among the writers on the subject
who have found it easier to ignore than to deal with the human
and other complexities of busing that the President addressed and
twisted to his own purposes in his speech and message. The busing
problem is real, it is national in scope, and there is a good though
certainly debatable case to be made for the solutions that the
President proposed, once he rid himself of the cheap simplicities
that marred his television speech. There could be no better illus-
tration of the importance of the terms in which public figures and
others define the busing issue, incidentally, than the event that
caused Mr. Nixon to change his original plan to let his message
speak for itself and decide, instead, to precede the message with a
prime-time television appearance. The event was the referendum
that accompanied the Florida primary on March 14. Floridians
voted 74 percent against compulsory busing and 79 percent for
desegregated (or "equal opportunity") public education. Only
voters conditioned to the false distinction between busing and
desegregation, by such masters of simplistic deception as Richard
Nixon and George C. Wallace, could have committed so complete
a contradiction. It is clear from the known sequence of intentions
at the White House that the Florida vote against compulsory busing presented the President with an irresistible temptation to ex-
ploit what he called "the highlights of the new approach I propose"
for political purposes.

The approach set forth in the message and draft legislation can
be properly evaluated and understood only if two assumptions
that underlie it and that Mr. Nixon elided to the point of conceal-
ment are understood. The first assumption is that the process of
legally required desegregation has been taken about as far as it
practically can be taken, both in the previously and overtly segregated South and in the urban North. The second assumption is

" WE DON'T STOP AT SCHOOLS ANYMORE..."

that, regardless of whether the first one is altogether justified, American society as a whole has had all of the required school desegregation that it is willing and prepared to tolerate for a while. Three specific and central Nixon proposals flow from these assumptions. The President asks Congress to enact a temporary ban upon all federal court orders for further busing. He asks that it permanently prohibit the further busing of children in the sixth grade and below, and allow the further busing of students in higher grades only when all other means of desegregation have been tested and found insufficient. He proposes that some $2 billion of federal money, from funds already authorized or requested, be concentrated annually upon improving the education delivered to disadvantaged pupils in schools that in his judgment could be desegregated only by extensive and (he assumes) intolerable busing. He makes other proposals, but the cited three comprise the core of his program.

The limitations that the President recommends are confined to "more busing" and "excessive busing." His package is cloaked in professions of dedication to continued desegregation; to "equal opportunity in education"; and to protection of related constitutional rights. But the series of White House briefing sessions that followed his speech and message removed any doubt I might have had that the President is in fact calling for a temporary halt to all effective school desegregation and for a permanent slowdown in every form of school desegregation. Mr. Nixon has never spoken or acted as if he believed that positive racial integration, in the schools and elsewhere, is a practical or desirable or imperative social and moral goal. Perhaps, this being so, it is idle to say that the President has abandoned any pretense to the contrary and has asked Congress and the nation to abandon it with him. But that is what has happened; that is what the President signaled with his busing message and legislation.

Secretary Richardson and others in a galaxy of White House briefers said, as the President did, that factual evidence supports the key proposition that a concentration of money and talent upon improving the education of isolated minority children will actually raise their levels of learning and performance. Inquiries at HEW indicated that this is true, but only marginally and debatably true. One of the shocking sleepers in the whole desegregation situation is the paucity of productive studies and believable data. Official, contract and academic students of desegregation and its corollaries are still gnawing at the carcass of the famous Coleman report, based in 1966 upon a study conducted in 1965 by Professor James Coleman and several associates. It remains the only comprehensive study, on a national scale, of segregation and desegregation and their consequences, social and educational. The proof that well-managed and well-financed compensatory effort has raised learning levels in some instances and may do it in others— the last is all that is really claimed—is thin and hasn't been adequately updated since 1969. After a decade of progressively effective desegregation in the South, HEW and its Office of Education have practically no solid evidence that desegregation as such does or does not raise the learning levels of minority children. The official conclusion, based on pathetically insufficient data, is that desegregation tends to bring "slightly positive educational change." HEW contractors are at work on two national studies that may remedy some of the lack, but one of them won't produce results for another two years and work on the other is slow.

It has been agreed here that Mr. Nixon didn't manufacture the busing problem. It must also be said, however, that his high-level briefers raised some questions as to whether the problem is as crucial and widespread as he says it is. Secretary Richardson, for instance, was asked whether a proposal to let southern and other school districts now under court and administrative busing orders reopen their cases if the standards set by Congress turn out to be milder than those presently imposed wouldn't undo much of the accomplished desegregation. No, he answered, because HEW and the courts have required much less busing than is generally supposed. The briefers were asked how many court decisions will be held in abeyance if the Nixon moratorium is voted. Richmond, Denver and Detroit, where drastic orders are in prospect or on appeal, were mentioned. Edward L. Morgan, a White House lawyer, said that in addition he could think of cases in Columbus, Augusta and Savannah, Ga.; Winston-Salem, NC; San Francisco; Tampa; and "a couple more." After Mr. Nixon's talk of a country "torn apart," answers of this kind had a rather troubling sound.

April 1, 1972

The 92nd Congress adjourned without enacting the President's anti-busing proposals. He and his assistants continued to mis-state the issue in terms of "racial balance" and compelled Elliot Richardson to join in the deception. Federal efforts to promote public school desegregation dwindled to the vanishing point. Expert studies casting doubt on the proposition that desegregated education is necessarily better than segregated education were welcomed with vocal joy at the Nixon White House.

X

President vs. Press

Mr. Nixon was looking mighty chipper when he strode into the Oval Office at nine minutes past three on the afternoon of March 24 and invited the reporters who had been called in without notice for the 23rd press conference of his presidency to fire away. He had on a powder-blue suit, beautifully pressed and not a wrinkle in it, a mildly startling departure from the darkish greys that he usually wears. Standing between his desk and the sun-lit windows at his back, with most of his weight on his right foot and his left leg slightly cocked over his right, he was tanned and smiling faintly and very much at ease when the questioning began. There were no cameras, no sound recorders except the one taking down the questions and answers for transcript purposes. It was strictly a notebook session, the second of the kind that the President has risked this year, a deliberate show of reliance upon the reporters to give fair and accurate accounts of what he said instead of addressing himself directly to the public over television and radio. Mr. Nixon answered, partly answered or refused to answer 21 questions in 30 minutes. At the end, when he sat down in his high-backed leather chair and opened an appointment book on his desk, he seemed to me to be noticeably tense and tired and I think I know why. Pretense does not come easily to Richard Nixon, however successfully he may indulge in it at times, and a performance that I judged to be skillful and effective on the whole must have been, for the President, an exhausting pretense at friendly and enjoyed exchange with the working press.

For authoritative evidence that the March 24 performance and others like it had to be exercises in pretense, I turned to my review copy of the first book about the Nixon White House to be written by a Nixon insider. The book is *President Nixon and the Press* (Funk & Wagnalls; $6.95). Its author is James Keogh, a former *Time* editor who was a special assistant to the President and the chief of the White House writing and research staff in 1969–70. It opens with an account of Nixon at a meeting with the members of his newly chosen Cabinet and their wives on December 12, 1968, the day after the President-elect introduced his appointees to the nation in a paid telecast. In galley proofs distributed by the publisher in January, "the essence" of what Nixon said to the group about their coming problems with the press appears as follows:

"Always remember, the men and women of the news media approach this as an adversary relationship. The time will come when they will run lies about you, when the columnists and editorial writers will make you seem to be scoundrels or fools or both and the cartoonists will depict you as ogres. Some of you wives will get up in the morning and look at the papers and start to cry. Now don't let this get you down—don't let it defeat you. And don't try to adjust your actions to what you think will please them. Do what you believe is the right thing to do and let the criticism roll off your back. Don't answer them in kind. Treat them as ladies and gentlemen. But you will find it difficult to deal with them as friends, no matter how well you may have known them."

It was to the last three sentences, the ones about ladies and gentlemen and friends, that I looked in the published book for my evidence. They are not in the published book. The following sentences appear in their place: "Don't think that the criticism you see or hear in one or two places is all that is getting through to the public. This is part of the process of communicating with the country and part of your job."

The thrust of Keogh's book and argument is that "Richard Nixon came to the Presidency not only without the support of most of the men and women who reported the news and commented on it, but with their active opposition." This attitude is attributed in part to personal prejudices and antipathies that had accumulated through Nixon's prior public years; in part to journalism's "historic obsession with the negative." But the serious argument, and it is a serious and documented argument, goes to what Keogh calls the "empathy" of most national journalists "for what is still best described, for all the over-use of the term, as the 'liberal' political philosophy." Keogh, whom I found to be a thoroughly conservative and decent and intelligent fellow when he was at the White House, disavows the corollary view that "there was a 'conspiracy' among journalists to control what the people saw and heard." He definitely does not disavow the most prominent exponent of the conspiratorial view, Vice President Agnew, but there are some refreshing acknowledgments, softly stated, that Agnew suffers from certain lacks of judgment and sensitivity. Keogh writes: "There was, of course, no conspiracy. There was a condition—a condition of conformity in which the most important and influential news media in the United States tended to report and comment on the news in a way which favored one political-philosophical point of view."

To all of which I say: so there was and so there is and so what? It is quite true, as Keogh asserts and shows at boring length, that most of the reporters who regularly cover the Nixon White House and many of the commentators who pass upon Mr. Nixon's policies and actions simply do not like and trust the man any more than he likes and trusts them. Granting that a gap of politics and philosophy and personal interaction does lie between the President and most of the journalists who track and vex him, I doubt that the general coverage of the Nixon presidency has been as deeply affected and as seriously distorted as Keogh says it has. Richard Nixon has had a better run with the national media than Lyndon Johnson had during most of his presidency. John Kennedy resented much of the coverage that he got from journalists who were, as Keogh says with a touch of envy, biased toward him rather than against him. The aspect of this book that interests me most is the evidence in it of the loyalist myopia that afflicts the President's associates. They reject, they cannot recognize, the possibility that Mr. Nixon brings upon himself most of his troubles and dissatisfactions with the press.

CBS Correspondent Dan Rather is rebuked for characterizing Mr. Nixon's discussion of his decision to invade Cambodia with congressional leaders as "a dialogue of the deaf." Keogh writes that "those of us who sat in on the meetings found them to be quite the contrary, with most of the members of Congress who were there showing deep interest, receptivity and appreciation." Exactly: White House accounts of such meetings would sound less like "dialogues of the deaf" if evidence were offered that the President's guests ever differ with him. "Some media" are denounced for overplaying Nixon's remark in Denver that Charles Manson, a defendant who was then on trial in Los Angeles, "was guilty, directly or indirectly, of eight murders without reason." Keogh notes that the Nixon staff was at fault "for not admitting and correcting the slip more quickly and frankly" than it did. The point he misses is that Attorney General John Mitchell, Press Secretary Ronald Ziegler, domestic assistant John Ehrlichman, and several other Nixonites who heard the remark were incapable of grasping and admitting quickly to themselves the fact that their man had made a grievous boner,

Much is made in the book of the media's emphasis upon Mr. Nixon's law-and-order theme during his campaigning for Republican senators and representatives in 1970. It may be true that in all but one of his campaign speeches the President devoted more time to "war and peace, welfare reform, revenue sharing, the environment and other issues" than he did "to dissent and violence— which he also discussed in every speech." But the "large distortion" that Keogh accuses the media of perpetrating would have occurred if the reporters had been so befuddled as to subordinate Mr. Nixon's raucous calls for law-and-order to his more placid themes. The reporters put their emphasis precisely where the President put his, on the bids to the rabble that got and were intended to get the cheers.

Tell it like it is, Keogh instructs the press. He upholds the right and duty of the press to analyse and criticize. But the message that comes through his call for more straight reporting and less advocacy is: tell it like officialdom says it is.

April 8, 1972

———

In December of 1972 Keogh put aside a book of White House reminiscences that he was writing and accepted the President's offer to make him Director of the U.S. Information Agency.

XI

Through the Window

This is how the Nixon presidency looked during the fortnight or so preceding April 5, as it was viewed through the murky window that more or less opens on it from the White House press room. The view that the reporters assigned to the White House get through that window is distorted and imperfect, a play of shadows on the wall behind which Mr. Nixon and his army of assistants do their work. But it's the view that they presumably want to project, or at any rate do project.

The chief keeper of the window, Press Secretary Ronald Ziegler, has been asked since early March how the President first learned that Harold Geneen, the president of the International Telephone and Telegraph Corp., had agreed that one of its subsidiaries, the Sheraton Corporation of America, would underwrite up to $400,000 of the expense of holding the Republican National Convention in San Diego next August. It is a pertinent question for several reasons. Mr. Nixon forced the convention upon San Diego, which didn't want it, so that he could commute to it from the nearby Western White House at San Clemente and accept his expected renomination for a second term in his home state. Sheraton, a hotel chain, has two hotels in San Diego and is building a third. Geneen told the Senate Judiciary Committee that his agreement to guarantee part of the convention cost was contingent upon a promise that Mr. Nixon would stay at the new hotel, and thereby attract valuable publicity for it, when he came to San Diego for renomination. It's all tied in with the ugly suggestion, denied by all hands and not proven to date, that the ITT-Sheraton guarantee was somehow connected with the Justice Department's later decision to settle a major antitrust case in ITT's favor. Geneen agreed to guarantee Sheraton's part of the cost on May 12. A report that he had done so was published in San Diego on July 3. Republican Congressman Bob Wilson of San Diego confirmed the report on or around August 5. Two Nixon assistants who might have been expected to know about it by then are Robert H. Finch, a former lieutenant governor of California, and Herbert Klein, a former San Diego editor. In May, at about the time Geneen was committing Sheraton to the guarantee, they visited San Diego and passed the word that Mr. Nixon wanted the convention to be held there. Klein and Finch said that they didn't recall just how and when they learned of the Sheraton guarantee. They were certain only that they had never reported it to Mr. Nixon or discussed any aspect of the difficult job of raising the necessary money with him. That left the ball with Ziegler (the reporters having failed to ask Mr. Nixon about it at his March 24 press conference). Ziegler's answers on two occasions were that he didn't know just when the President learned of the ITT-Sheraton guarantee, but he did know that it was from one of the daily news summaries that the staff prepares for Mr. Nixon. When was that—before or after the Senate Judiciary Committee began its inquiry into the whole affair? "At the time it came to be in the news," Ziegler answered. Patrick Buchanan, the assistant who supervises preparation of the news summary, found on page 26 of the one for November 30 a long paragraph conveying to the President (if he read it and Buchanan wasn't sure that he had) the essence of a story that had appeared the day before in the *Washington Evening Star*. It was a thorough job by Robert Walters, a *Star* investigative reporter, and Mr. Nixon should have realized after reading the barest summary of it that bad trouble for him was lurking in the ITT situation.

Whether he realized it and how he reacted if he did remain unknown, except that he visibly did nothing whatever to forestall the storm. Two little facts, the kind that illumine the shadows on the wall, did emerge. One of them is that the President's news

ITT MEMO SHREDDER

1972, The Register
and Tribune Syndicate ©THE LOS ANGELES TIMES, 1972.

CONRAD

summarizers usually don't digest reports in *The New York Times* and *The Washington Post* because "he reads those papers for himself." The other one is that some of the President's advisers are suggesting that he get around the embarrassment of putting up at the new Sheraton hotel in San Diego by letting it be known as "the Nixon hotel" without staying in it. He can hop from San Clemente to San Diego by helicopter, deliver his acceptance speech, return to his California home for the night, and if necessary repeat the shuttle when his choice for Vice President is nominated. The Nixon stamp can be affixed to the hotel by having some of his assistants lodge there and maybe making it the headquarters of his Committee for the Reelection of the President.

The Committee for the Reelection of the President figures frequently in the press room play. The reporters hear of it whenever they ask what the President calls "partisan political questions." Ziegler refers such questions to the committee, frankly identifying it for what it is—an extension of the Nixon White House. Its employes, totaling 125 at last count and growing in number by the day, are quartered a block from the White House, on Pennsylvania Avenue, on two floors and pieces of several others in the building where the former Nixon law firm has its Washington offices. Former Attorney General John N. Mitchell, who is to be the Nixon campaign director, has rejoined the firm and has two offices on the fourth floor of the building, one for his law practice and one for his campaign duties. His wife, Martha, is a committee volunteer and has been allotted a nook on an upper floor. A reporter, noting that Mr. Nixon had answered a question about political contributions at his last press conference, asked Ziegler the other day why his policy and the President's policy on answering political questions seem to differ. "I didn't know it did," Ziegler said, and evaded the difficulty by saying the President had answered *that* question and he, the press secretary, wasn't going to answer it again or answer any others like it. The White House telephone operators gladly give inquirers the committee number (333-0920) but won't put outsiders' calls through to the committee offices.

A burning issue in the press room was whether the North Vietnamese offensive in South Vietnam, with the questions it raises

about further American troop withdrawals and about the success
of Nixon Vietnamization, had created a crisis at the White House.
Reporter to Ziegler: "Do you notice any crisis atmosphere around
here?" Ziegler to reporter: "I haven't noticed that around here,
but I notice that some reporters have noticed that." A classic
example of the answers White House reporters get was provided
by Deputy Press Secretary Gerald Warren when he was asked
whether the President's acknowledged "concern" about the situation had led to some decisions, and he replied: "The review [of
the war situation] is under way; the President is reviewing it; his
advisers are reviewing it; and we are awaiting the results of that
review." Observing that most of the substantial comment and of
what passed for news about the President's reaction to the war
events was coming from the State Department rather than the
White House, a reporter asked Ziegler, "Is that an attempt to keep
the focus off the President at this time of non-crisis?" Ziegler
answered in effect: don't be ridiculous, the State Department was
the proper place for the answers to come from. It was perfectly
natural, he maintained, for him to be consulting daily with Robert
McCloskey, the department spokesman, who proved himself to be
a cool and competent expounder of official views years before
Ziegler arrived in Washington. Their common line, set at the
White House, was that the North Vietnamese attack across the
Demilitarized Zone was a "flagrant violation" of past accords and,
in Ziegler's favorite term, a "blatant" offense against the known
proprieties. The President has implied since the Vietnam war became his war that there is something uniquely sinful in North
Vietnam's persistent attempts to win it, and that was the dominant
thought that Mr. Nixon had his spokesmen try to encourage.

The press staff let reporters assume as late as March 30 that the
President was going to visit Ft. Campbell in Kentucky during the
first week of April to celebrate the withdrawal of the 101st Air-
borne Division from Vietnam. On April 3, it was said that the
President never had decided to go to Ft. Campbell and wasn't
going. Had he changed his mind because of the Vietnam situation?
Not at all, the answer came; it was just "a matter of the President's scheduling."

———

A North Vietnamese attack on South Vietnam, across the Demilitarized Zone that divides North and South Vietnam, began on
March 31 and required no explicit reference when the foregoing
report was written. The President's immediate response with increased air and naval bombardment of North Vietnam similarly
required no explicit reference in the above and following reports.

XII

Baiting Moscow

The first official reference to the Soviet Union in connection with the North Vietnamese offensives in South Vietnam occurred at the State Department on April 3, in response to a reporter's question. The question was whether the department detected a relationship between the attacks and "the presence in Hanoi last week of an extremely high-level Soviet military delegation." Robert McCloskey, who usually works in private as Secretary of State William P. Rogers' personal spokesman and on White House orders had temporarily taken over the daily department press briefing, answered "I can't say; I don't know." The next day, in the course of complaining that South Vietnam was the victim of "a naked attack by regular units of the North Vietnamese military," McCloskey dropped the following remark: "And I wish to call to your attention that these units are supported in a very large way by heavy military equipment from the Soviet Union." Why, he was asked, did he wish to call that fact to the attention of the press? "To emphasize the nature of this attack," he replied. His point, stated in the tone of a prosecutor accusing a defendant of heinous crime, was that the Soviet supply of tanks, anti-aircraft missiles and the like to the North Vietnamese had made possible "a divergence from the more traditional pattern of guerrilla warfare to conventional warfare." McCloskey conceded that the Communist

Chinese, whom he hadn't mentioned, had been supplying North Vietnam with weapons for many years. But "the more massive use of heavy equipment—which traditionally has come from the Soviet Union—adds a new factor to the situation on the battlefield in South Vietnam." Was he suggesting that Soviet participation went beyond military supply to a "larger role in the offensive, in the planning or political considerations?" McCloskey answered, "I think that would be speculative now," and said in response to another question that he wasn't trying to promote speculation "in that direction."

So began the baiting of Moscow that played a part in the preparation of the American public for the vastly expanded use of US air and naval power, in South and North Vietnam, to support South Vietnam's ground forces. Defense Secretary Melvin Laird and his spokesmen at the Pentagon hit the Soviet gong often and hard. But it fell to McCloskey, a deft and experienced purveyor of the official line, to handle the nuances of the game devised for him and other administration spokesmen in daily consultations at the White House. The problem was how to make the most of a suggestion of Soviet responsibility without letting it grow into provocative accusation that might offend the Soviet government beyond endurance and imperil President Nixon's trip to Moscow in late May. McCloskey didn't have to volunteer further digs at the Soviet Union. Once he had manufactured the issue with his original remark, the reporters kept it alive with questions.

When he was asked whether the trip was in jeopardy, McCloskey first answered: "There is no reconsideration of the projected visit of the President to the Soviet Union." In subsequent replies, after further consultation at the White House, he took a subtly qualified line that left open the implied possibility that the President might call off the trip if Soviet behavior in the meantime and Soviet attitudes to be expected in Moscow didn't suit him. A typical answer in the reconsidered phase was, "I have no reason to understand [that] the preparations for the trip are not going ahead as planned and I have no reason to expect that it will not take place as scheduled." An advance party would be going to Moscow ahead of the President, but a date for its departure hadn't been set and it would be "low level . . . not at a policy level." A daily question put to McCloskey was whether the US government had officially complained or intended to complain to the Soviet

government about its military aid to Hanoi. His standard reply—
"I don't know the answer to that at this point"—left that possibility similarly open without committing anybody to anything. An
admission that the US didn't have much to complain about was
implicit in one of the exchanges. McCloskey was asked, "Have we
had a tacit understanding with the Soviet Union that the heavy
equipment supplied Hanoi would not be used below the Demilitarized Zone?" and he answered "No." Asked again why he had
brought up the matter of Soviet supply, especially since he had
boasted that US intelligence services had been "on the money" in
foreseeing the attacks, he said that he had brought it up because
"it was a statement of relevant fact that we thought it was important to know and to say publicly."

At the White House, the President's staff spokesmen went to
comical lengths to keep him detached from the exercise during its
first seven days. Their refusals to acknowledge that he was directing the military response to the North Vietnamese attacks, much
less setting the propaganda line, invited but didn't elicit from the
press a question as to whether he had abdicated to others his
duties and responsibilities as the nation's Commander-in-Chief. Of
course he hadn't, and he cut through the flimflam at the State
Department on April 10 when he signed a convention barring the
use of bacteriological weapons. In the presence of Soviet Ambassador Anatoliy Dobrynin, the President made occasion to say
that "every great power must follow the principle that it should
not encourage directly or indirectly any other nation to use force
or armed aggression against one of its neighbors." Press Secretary
Ronald Ziegler said afterward, "I am not going to assist you in
applying those remarks." No assistance was needed: the Presient's
statement capped the week-long indictment of the Soviet Union
and effectively identified him as its author.

A cynical explanation could be that Richard Nixon, the avid
anti-Communist and Red-hunter of bygone years, simply couldn't
pass up the opportunity, even in this year of climactic conciliation,
to have another shot at Moscow. Maybe there was a bit of that in
it, not to mention the President's dire need for any line that could
divert attention from the fact that after seven years of intensive
American involvement in the Vietnam war and three years of

Nixon Vietnamization the North Vietnamese still had the strength
to mount a formidable offensive and the South Vietnamese still
required a prodigious amount of supporting US firepower in order
to survive. But there is a more generous and probably more relevant explanation, one that better fits the pattern of expressed
Nixon attitudes toward the Soviet Union since he opened his "era
of negotiation" in 1969.

The record demonstrates that the President takes pleasure and
sees value in his endeavor to instruct the Soviet leadership in the
conduct that he thinks fitting for a great power. In the three annual summations of his foreign policy that he has issued to date,
his references to the Soviet Union are replete with the kind of
admonitions that he addressed to Moscow on April 10. Henry
Kissinger, his staff adviser, subscribes with fervent enthusiasm to
the theory that these preachments do some good and is the framer
of many of them. In a press briefing last December 7 that was
supposed to be off the record and got on the record, Kissinger set
forth as follows the precept that he and Mr. Nixon would like to
impress upon the Soviet Union: "We believe that the basis of a
peaceful evolution with the Soviet Union requires that both countries [meaning the USSR and the US] exercise great restraint in
the many crisis areas around the world and that they both subordinate short-term advantages to the long-term interests of
peace." This was said during the India-Pakistan conflict, in the
course of which Kissinger inspired a news report to the effect that
the President's Moscow trip might be cancelled and "the entire US-
Soviet relationship" might have to be reexamined if the Soviet
government didn't stop exploiting the situation for its own benefit.
On April 10 and in the preceding week, he and the President were
saying to Moscow that in the US view the Soviet government was
again playing for "short-term advantage" and again risking a rup-
ture with the United States by continuing to support and encourage Hanoi's prosecution of the war. What seemed to many people
to be frivolous and dangerous reversion to Cold War semantics
was, in the estimate of the President and his adviser, a serious and
necessary effort to condition the Soviet leadership for a productive
meeting with Mr. Nixon in May.

April 22, 1972

XIII

Spring Maneuvers

While the bombers were prowling over North Vietnam and Mr. Nixon was exchanging jollities with the table tennis players from Communist China in the Rose Garden, workmen were busy at the main entrance to the White House on Pennsylvania Avenue. They were beefing up the array of bullet-proof windows, steel panels and electrically controlled slots which minimize the chances that disgruntled citizens might try to blow up the police cubicle at the Northwest Gate. This activity was the only sign of apprehension that the President's escalation of American air and naval warfare in Vietnam might have undesirable and uncontrollable consequences. The conveyed impression was that Mr. Nixon was doing only what he's been saying since 1969 that he'd do if the enemy took advantage of his moves to wind down the Indochina war and that, when it is all over, his conduct of the war and his dealings with Peking and Moscow will be seen to constitute a triumph of presidential judgment and statesmanship.

The ultimate commentary upon the state of the world in 1972 is that the conveyed impression may turn out to be correct. If it does, it will be because the leaders in Hanoi, Peking and Moscow with whom Mr. Nixon is dealing and fencing are as cynical and ruthless in the pursuit of their aims as he is proving himself to be

in the pursuit of his aims. In their revulsion against the renewed
horrors of American air and naval bombardment that the President has loosed upon both Vietnams, the critics of his policy and
actions will do themselves and the cause of peace a disservice if
they fail to face and recognize the facts that he faced and manipu-
lated and in part had brought about as of April 20. North Vietnam's military forces, armed by the Soviet Union as they have
never before been armed, were fighting in most of South Vietnam
at a level and in a fashion that they have never before attempted
to sustain. The North Vietnamese and US governments were urging each other to resume open or secret peace talks in Paris and
each government was saying to the other that it would do so only
on its terms and when free of the military pressure to which each
was subjecting the other. Hanoi's principal supporters and sup-
pliers, the Soviet Union and the People's Republic of China, were
continuing to welcome Mr. Nixon's moves toward accommodation
with them while verbally deploring his escalated attacks upon
North Vietnam. The ,day after the Chinese table tennis team and
the President swapped smiles and handshakes at the White House,
Premier Chou En-lai was heard on NBC television, praising the
Nixon approach to rapprochement with the People's Republic.
After the President twice accused the Soviet Union of responsibility for the North Vietnamese attacks upon South Vietnam, and
while some people were wondering whether and when the Soviet
leaders would cancel their scheduled summit conference with him
in Moscow, the Polish ambassador in Washington appeared at the
White House and cordially invited Mr. Nixon to visit Warsaw on
his way home. After State and Defense Secretaries Rogers and
Laird repeated the accusation of Soviet responsibility in abrasive
and insulting terms, and the State Department spelled out the
charge in a diplomatic note rejecting Moscow's complaint that
four Russian ships had been damaged by American bombs and
rockets in Haiphong harbor, the advance party preparing the
Nixon visit arrived in Moscow and got down to work with Soviet
officials.

The crazy pattern of action and response did not justify—
nothing could justify—the President's extension of the bombing
and shelling from the theaters of close engagement in South Vietnam to the cities and hamlets of North Vietnam and his threat of
unlimited bombing short only of nuclear attack. But, in the prag-

matic and amoral terms that prevail at the Nixon White House, it did justify and explain the controlling assumption that nothing the President does in Indochina is likely to upset his grand design for accommodation with the pragmatists in Peking and Moscow.

Anonymous leakers at the Pentagon told a *New York Times* reporter that Secretary Laird doubted the wisdom and necessity of bombing Hanoi and Haiphong. James Reston of that journal reported that Henry Kissinger advised the President to cut down the propaganda emphasis upon Soviet aid to Hanoi. If so, the advice was ignored, and both reports smacked of the tendency in this and all administrations for individuals to protect their reputations just in case a risky policy goes wrong. The assumption itself, the details of applying it aside, was pure Kissinger. One of his tenets has been that a Communist invitation to summitry with an American President is evidence that the host government—Peking last February, Moscow in May—considers negotiation at the top to be in its fundamental and compelling interest. Once the invitation has been issued and accepted, Kissinger is known to reason, each party to the pending summitry has at least an equal interest in seeing that nothing is allowed to prevent the consummation. The President and Kissinger, to the extent that he guided the President's course before the Peking meeting, were much more wary in testing the theory then than they are being now with the Moscow government. Then the greatest care was taken that nothing be done or said that could possibly offend the Chinese leadership. The current brinksmanship with Moscow suggests that the Soviet government's interest in bringing off a successful summit with Mr. Nixon is assumed to be so compelling that Brezhnev and Kosygin will tolerate almost anything rather than call off the meeting.

April 29, 1972

XIV

White House Nerves

Here is the recent record of how the President got himself where he was in the first week of May, facing the defeat in Vietnam that he was still saying he'd never accept.

On March 23, Ambassador William J. Porter told the North Vietnamese and Vietcong negotiators in Paris that the US was suspending the abortive peace talks until it had "some sign from you that you are disposed to engage in meaningful exchanges." Mr. Nixon said in Washington the next day that "this has been done under my direction" because "we are not going to continue to allow them to use this forum for the purpose of bullyragging the United States in a propaganda forum rather than in seriously negotiating peace." He also said, "I am not saying that this move is going to bring a negotiation. I do say, however, that it was necessary to do something to get the talks off dead center" and added, "When they are ready, we are ready." The President didn't mention and the press generally overlooked a reference in Ambassador Porter's Paris statement to "road-building activities clearly designed for offensive purposes" in the Demilitarized Zone which separates North and South Vietnam.

The North Vietnamese army moved across the DMZ into South

Vietnam with infantry, tanks and artillery on March 30 and 31. Through the following week, Nixon spokesmen denounced this "naked attack" and "massive invasion" and repeatedly indicated that the US would not resume open or secret peace talks so long as the offensive continued. Then it developed that on April 1, the day the scale of the North Vietnamese attack first became apparent, the President secretly offered to resume the Paris sessions on April 6. The North Vietnamese in Paris said, and events confirmed, that within two or three days after making the offer the President withdrew it. Feeble evasions amounted to an admission that he had offered to resume negotiations upon condition that the North Vietnamese halt their offensive and pull back across the DMZ.

In Paris and Hanoi, North Vietnamese officials and spokesmen said almost daily that they were ready and anxious to resume negotiation whenever Mr. Nixon was. In Washington, two lines of thought were publicly and privately encouraged. One was that the enemy offensive, by then spreading from the northern provinces of South Vietnam to other parts of the country, could not be sustained very long under renewed and escalated American air and naval attack. The other line of encouraged speculation was that the North Vietnamese were lavishly and foolishly spending their resources in a gamble aimed at positioning themselves to negotiate a favorable settlement. In this sense, the enemy show of strength was said to be a welcomed prelude to the "serious negotiation" that the President and his adviser, Henry Kissinger, had hoped to bring about with the suspension of the Paris talks in March.

The President ordered the bombing of Haiphong harbor and the outskirts of Hanoi on April 16. Four Soviet ships were hit and (it later became known) one was sunk. On April 18, the day the President greeted a Communist Chinese table tennis team at the White House, Henry Kissinger canceled his afternoon appointments and vanished. On the following Tuesday, one week later, he reappeared at the White House and Press Secretary Ronald Ziegler announced that the US had agreed to resume the plenary peace talks in Paris, stipulating that "the first item of business in these talks must be the discussion of measures which will put an end to the flagrant North Vietnamese invasion of South Vietnam." Kissinger, it was also announced, had been secretly in Moscow from Thursday the 20th to Monday the 24th, conferring with Party

Chairman Leonid Brezhnev and Foreign Minister Andrei Gromyko. Kissinger said that he had not gone to Moscow "to save" the President's scheduled summit conference there in late May, but to enhance the chances of successful talks and felt that his visit had given them "additional impetus." During three press appearances in two days, he refused to say while clearly implying that Brezhnev and Gromyko had encouraged him to believe that useful negotiations with the North Vietnamese would now be possible. Kissinger said that "we have this expectation" and should know before the President arrives in Moscow on May 22 "whether we are talking [with the North Vietnamese] in terms of propositions which make a settlement possible." He also said that "it is our position" that the North Vietnamese must withdraw from South Vietnam the forces that had recently crossed the DMZ, but he stopped short of making this a condition to the resumption of either plenary talks or secret negotiations of the kind that he had conducted with Le Duc Tho, a senior Hanoi minister, from August of 1969 to September 1971. Kissinger noted press reports that Tho was about to go from Hanoi to Paris and remarked that "he does not generally return for trivial reasons." The effect was to promote the supposition that Kissinger would soon and again be in negotiation with Tho, privately and apart from the plenary Paris sessions.

Mr. Nixon strengthened the supposition when he said, in the course of announcing his intention to withdraw another 20,000 American troops from South Vietnam by July 1: "We are resuming the Paris talks with the firm expectation that productive talks leading to rapid progress will follow through all available channels." In the rest of his speech, televised the night of the 26th, he talked as if he were inviting the North Vietnamese *not* to negotiate. His renewed bombings of North Vietnam would continue "until the invasion stops." Letting the North Vietnamese have their way in South Vietnam would be to destroy "the respect that is essential" for "the President of the United States" and "to deny peace the chance that peace deserves to have." And: "This we shall never do." At a Sunday assemblage of Texas wealth and power on Treasury Secretary John B. Connally's ranch near San Antonio, the President repeated and amplified these bombastics, with emphasis upon his resolve to tear North Vietnam to shreds if that were necessary to "do the job."

Tho arrived in Paris, after stops in Peking and Moscow, on April 30. An airport statement repeated in essence the North Vietnamese terms that in the President's judgment had always called for surrender of South Vietnam to the Communists. But Tho did it in pacific language. In spirit though not in substance, he seemed to echo Kissinger's similarly hopeful and conciliatory tone and to be telling the President's adviser that the "expectation" of substantive negotiation was justified. Secretary of State William P. Rogers said on "Meet the Press" that Tho's statement was "no way to negotiate a settlement" and a State Department spokesman said it was "a disappointment." Kissinger vanished briefly on May 1 and 2, then turned up again with the President on a night cruise down the Potomac, and his staff indicated that he was at the White House on May 3. The first of the resumed plenary sessions in Paris produced nothing but renewed and mutual vilification. The disintegration of South Vietnam's military forces in the northern provinces became so obvious and proceeded so far that a Defense Department spokesman had to acknowledge that the situation was "serious." The President, who had said in Texas that the North Vietnamese "can make their own choice" between halting their attacks and exposing themselves to more "strikes on military targets throughout North Vietnam," had a choice of his own to make. It was whether to negotiate at once for whatever he could save from the wreckage of Vietnamization, or again to escalate and rely upon the bombing that has always failed to "do the job" in Indochina.

May 13, 1972

———

Vietnamization was not wrecked and the President continued to rely upon the bombing. His televised speech of May 8, announcing maximum reliance on bombing and harbor mining, preceded the following report.

XV

At the Brink

During the 15 minutes that the President spent in the Cabinet Room at the White House with Democratic and Republican leaders of Congress, telling them what he had decided to do in Vietnam before he told the country and the world, he permitted no discussion and no questions. He recited the gist of the speech that he was about to make on television and said in conclusion: "If you can give me your support, I will appreciate it. If you cannot, I will understand." Mike Mansfield of Montana, the Senate majority leader, had brought along a written report on the trip to Communist China that he and Senator Hugh Scott of Pennsylvania, the Republican leader, had just completed. Mansfield handed the report to the President, who said that he would try to read it later that night. Then, a little tense but smiling slightly and saying that he had to prepare to go on camera in 45 minutes, he left the shaken leaders with Secretary of Defense Melvin Laird, Secretary of State William P. Rogers, and Admiral Thomas H. Moorer, Jr., the chairman of the Joint Chiefs of Staff.

Henry Kissinger was not there—he was with Soviet Ambassador Anatoliy Dobrynin, telling him what the President was about to say. Mansfield and Senator J. William Fulbright, the foreign relations committee chairman, put the questions that they were given no chance to ask the President to Moorer, Laird and Rogers. The questions were tough, hostile, shot through with the doubts of both the necessity and wisdom of the President's course that were soon expressed in public. Senator Scott, Congressman Gerald Ford and the other Republicans present had very little to say. Laird, alert to the political overtones, frequently moved in on Admiral Moorer and dealt as best he could with the doubts that the steps to be announced and already ordered by the President— mining the entrances to the harbors of North Vietnam, bombing and shelling its coasts and bombing the railway lines that bring Soviet and Chinese supplies into North Vietnam from Communist China—made either military or diplomatic sense. Rogers concentrated upon the challenge to the Soviet Union that the President was about to proclaim. The Secretary of State argued that the challenge was not quite as arrant, not quite as dangerous, not quite as likely to wreck the Moscow summit conference scheduled to begin in two weeks as he, Rogers, knew it would at first appear to be. He presented a lawyer's oral brief to the effect that the mining and the other naval measures to interdict the delivery of seaborne Soviet supplies did not amount either legally or actually to a blockade, with the complexities and dangers that a declared blockade would entail. The President had taken care, Rogers said, that there need be no open confrontation with Soviet naval or merchant vessels on the high seas. Everything was to be done on North Vietnamese territory and, as the President was to say, "within the internal and claimed territorial waters of North Vietnam."

After Mr. Nixon delivered his speech, he met with the assembled Cabinet. Among its members, only Rogers, Laird and Treasury Secretary John B. Connally had been told what the President was going to do and say. Rogers, it appears, had been informed on the previous day when he was suddenly recalled from Europe, where he had been making the rounds of NATO governments and telling their heads of the President's high hopes for historic summit agreements in Moscow on strategic arms limitations, US and Soviet cooperation in space exploration, and expanded US-Soviet trade. At the Cabinet meeting, the Nixon message was gently but tersely stated. This speech, the President said, was one that he had written himself. The decisions announced in it were his decisions, they had been made, and there was to be no hedging on them, no

"SOMEDAY, PRESIDENT THIEU, ALL THIS WILL BE YOURS!"

backing off from them, by anybody in his presence or in the administration. The understood implication was that he didn't want to see in the newspapers or hear on the air of any self-serving reservations, any dissents that might have been expressed to him or within lower councils. The same message was passed, more by osmosis than by explicit order, to the White House staff. The impression conveyed to press and public was to be that the risks so clearly taken by the President had been taken calmly, after cool deliberation; not in anger and not in frustration, and not with any sense of impending defeat in Vietnam.

These last were absurd instructions, impossible to fulfill. They could not be believed of a President who had said on television, after reeling off a litany of offered concessions to the Communist enemy: "And North Vietnam has met each of these offers with insolence and insult. They have flatly and arrogantly refused to negotiate an end of the war and bring peace. . . . And now, as throughout the past four years, the North Vietnamese arrogantly refuse to negotiate anything but an imposition, an ultimatum, that the United States impose a Communist regime on 17 million people in South Vietnam who do not want a Communist government." Henry Kissinger, holding forth for an hour to reporters at the White House the next day, displayed with flushed face and trembling voice a profound sense of anger and indignation. His and the President's expressed anger was directed chiefly at the North Vietnamese negotiators in Paris who had rebuffed Kissinger when he flew there secretly for a meeting on May 2. His and Mr. Nixon's feelings toward the Soviet leaders with whom Kissinger conferred in Moscow on April 20–24, also in secret, and with whom the President still hoped to meet in Moscow on May 22, had to be deduced from what the President and his adviser said and from the ways in which they said it. My deduction follows.

The President felt, and wanted the Soviet leaders to know he felt, that they had led him down the garden path. He blamed them for inducing Kissinger to induce him to resume suspended negotiations in Paris, with what Kissinger in Moscow had judged to be persuasive indications if not an outright promise that they would encourage the Hanoi government to withdraw sufficiently from its past demands to make an early settlement of the war possible on terms that the President could accept without appearing to surrender South Vietnam to immediate Communist rule. And Kissinger discovered in Paris, as he and the President said, that the North Vietnamese still demanded all that they had previously demanded and offered nothing that they had not previously offered. Kissinger acknowledged that the Soviet government's ability to influence and restrain the Hanoi government was probably not "very great." The President, addressing himself to the Soviet leaders, acknowledged that "we expect you to help your allies." But he held them responsible for helping their Vietnamese allies "to launch invasions against their neighbors" and, in the larger context of his and the Soviet approaches toward "a new relationship," for failure to achieve that relationship if the beginnings of it were now to founder upon his challenge in Vietnam. When the President said, "We do not ask you to sacrifice your principles or friends. But neither should you permit Hanoi's intransigence to blot out the prospects we together have so patiently prepared," he aborted Kissinger's claim of reasoned awareness, even in anger, that the capacity of the Soviet leaders to permit or forbid the Hanoi leadership to do anything is distinctly limited.

In his press appearance after the President spoke, Kissinger gave every sign of total support for the decision to elevate this miserable war, this regional conflict, to the level of declared confrontation with the Soviet Union and of tacit confrontation with the People's Republic of China. This he did with an accompanying and appropriate show of humility. Since 1969, he has misjudged and underestimated the endurance of the North Vietnamese and Vietcong Communists and overestimated their readiness, at some juncture, to negotiate a settlement on terms less than terms that he rightly perceives to be a victor's terms. He came close to confessing as much when he said in answer to a question: "Do I still believe that there is hope for negotiations? I have always based my hope of negotiations on the fact [sic] that even in Vietnam there must be some realities that transcend the parochial concerns of the contestants and that a point must be reached where a balance is so clearly established that, if we can make generous and far-seeing proposals, a solution may be possible."

May 20, 1972

XVI

Ready for Moscow

The week of May 15 was one of the times when the observer of the Nixon presidency could only sit back, mildly stunned, and marvel at its workings. Mr. Nixon let his wife say first and officially that he was going to Moscow after all, thereby suggesting that the previous show of uncertainty that his prospective Soviet hosts would still welcome him to the summit was either pretense or a confession that the President and his adviser, Henry Kissinger, had been playing in frivolous doubt and ignorance with the fate of mankind when they confronted the Soviet government with the challenge posed to it in Vietnam. The President and an associate now revealed to have been a strong advocate of the turn in Vietnam policy, Secretary of the Treasury John B. Connally, asked the public to believe that they had known all along what literally nobody else in the administration seemed to know—namely, that Connally had arranged to quit before or around this time when he joined the Cabinet in December 1970. His resignation was announced the day after George C. Wallace was shot in a Washington suburb, a short drive from the White House, and Mr. Nixon managed with perfect grace and propriety to precede the disclosure of Connally's impending departure with a demonstration of a President's unique power to act in a politically advantageous way while other candidates for the office could only bemoan the event. With Connally and his intended successor, Budget Director

George P. Shultz, standing beside him in the White House press room, Mr. Nixon said that he had offered Wallace the presidential suite at Walter Reed Hospital in Washington for his recuperation or, if he preferred, an Air Force hospital plane to take him home to Alabama. It was a decent thing to do, and it was unlikely to repel Wallace voters to whom Mr. Nixon also appeals on such divisive issues as school busing.

Connally, enjoying the astonishment that his leaving caused, said in his Texas drawl that he was sure it "will raise questions in the minds of many," and it did. It also provided the latest testimony to the extraordinary ability of Mr. Nixon and of men whom he trusts to keep their secrets until they are ready to reveal the versions they want to put about. In interviews with several reporters during the previous week, all of them doing stories on Connally as a key and continuing member of the Nixon Cabinet, he didn't hint that he was about to quit. At a meeting of most of Mr. Nixon's political advisers and assistants the night before the announcement, nobody present indicated the slightest knowledge that the speculation about Connally's role in the Nixon campaign for reelection was going to be stimulated so soon and in so spectacular a way. The thrust of the speculation was that Mr. Nixon was getting set to dump Vice President Agnew from the 1972 Republican ticket and replace him with Connally, the only Democrat in the Cabinet and one of the few vivid characters in this drab administration. Connally said that it was "entirely possible" that he'd be supporting the Nixon candidacy; that he expected to be mighty busy in the summer and fall (after the party conventions); and that he wouldn't discuss such a remote possibility as his being on the Republican ticket with Nixon. The impression left by a master contriver of impressions was that it is indeed a possibility.

It's all speculation and nothing more at this stage, and I might as well throw out my own contribution. It is founded upon a conviction, derived from many accounts over the years of the corrosive personal effects that Mr. Nixon's defeats in 1960 and 1962 had upon him, that he will never knowingly invite another defeat. His talk, in interviews and in other remarks this year, has been studded with indications of an inner awareness that he may have very little time in the presidency left to him and that in all he does he is preparing the way for future Presidents and perhaps for the next President—"whoever he may be," Mr. Nixon has said in the course of saying that one of his chief purposes is to preserve "respect for the office of President of the United States." So, getting to a point that is laughed at when I mention it around the White House, I find myself wondering whether Richard Nixon may be setting up John Bowden Connally, just in case, to be the next Republican nominee for the presidency. Connally, by repeated avowal a committed Nixocrat, has all but read himself out of the Democratic Party. With his bold conservative stance, he is assured of a warmer welcome at the Republican convention in August than he could expect to get at the Democratic convention in July. The President said in announcing the resignation that he has some special assignments in mind for Connally and that the first of them will be disclosed after the return from Moscow. Inviting one and all to laugh away, I leave it at that.

The serious business at the White House was the preparation for Moscow and the ceremonial stops on the way home at Warsaw and Teheran. Henry Kissinger, publicly silent and all but invisible since he surfaced in the East Room on May 9th to explain and justify the policy of escalation and confrontation announced by the President on the 8th, said then that the recognized risk of serious confrontation with Moscow was judged to be "not unacceptable." The superficial risk, the one generally discussed in the press, was that Soviet officialdom might withdraw its invitation to meet at the summit with Mr. Nixon in Moscow on May 22 and through the following week rather than accept the humiliation implicit in his steps to bar, with naval and aerial force, the further shipment of Soviet war supplies to North Vietnam. The greater risks, in diminishing order of likelihood, were that pending and long-prepared US-Soviet agreements on strategic arms limitation, trade expansion, the status of West Berlin, and space cooperation might have been negated just when they were about to be affirmed and made final at the Moscow summit; and that the Soviet Union might reply with force to Mr. Nixon's measures of force. One effect of the verbal confrontation, certainly not wanted by either party, was to expose the symbolic nature of the Moscow conference. It suddenly became apparent that the agreements in question could be completed, and that the subsequent negotiation of remaining issues could occur, whether or not the President was received in Moscow. This appeared to be the fall-back hope and assumption entertained by the President and Kissinger during the brief period of professed uncertainty. Lacking sure knowledge either way, I doubt that the uncertainty was ever as great as it was allowed to seem. My hunch is that Nixon and Kissinger were never in substantial doubt that they would be leaving for Moscow on schedule.

Why, if this supposition be correct, the inspired indications from Kissinger's vicinity that the chances for a time were 9-to-1 against the trip occurring? Why the delay in the announcement of press and other travel arrangements that were nearly complete when the President spoke and were finally dribbled to concerned journalists a full week after they were to have been published? It was all, if my supposition is correct, a way of letting the Moscow government appear to be the controlling partner in the preliminaries to the summit. It was a ploy in a deadly serious game for a better and safer world that the US, Soviet and Communist Chinese governments are playing with each other. The extreme extension of this supposition is that, in the cynical phrase tossed around Washington last week, "the fix is on" between the US and Communist China and between the US and the Soviet Union. This I do not believe. What I do believe and assume is that an exchange of judgments, a process of mutually encouraged impression, is occurring at the peaks of the US, Peking and Moscow leaderships. The shared judgment thus arrived at and in process of being arrived at is that the supreme interests of the great powers outweigh in importance to each of them and to the world the lesser ties and obligations (Mr. Nixon's to Saigon, Moscow's and Peking's to Hanoi) that have constrained and motivated them. At this writing, before he departs for Moscow, the President appears to be giving more support to Saigon than Moscow and Peking are giving to Hanoi. But that could change and, after Moscow and despite all the evidence to the contrary, it may begin to change sooner and to better purpose than seems possible now. On of the facts about Mr. Nixon that his critics ought to grasp is that he is least credible when he says such things as that he will never, never sell out to the Communists in South Vietnam. He will, when and if he is offered terms that he judges to be to his country's and the world's advantage.

May 27, 1972

———

My lightsome speculation about John Connally's future proved to be un-laughably wrong in 1972, though it may appear to be quite right in 1976. My interpretation of the preludes to the Moscow visit stood up very well.

XVII

The Pressure of Fear

Moscow

The Soviet journalists who are assigned to spend their evening hours with the reporters in the President's press party find it easier to answer the question that we are continually asking them than we find it to answer the question that they ask us most often and with the greatest intensity. Our question is, why was Mr. Nixon allowed to come to Moscow after he affronted and aggrieved the Soviet government with his Vietnam speech on May 8, and the actions that he took and is still taking to bar Soviet military and other supplies from North Vietnam with military force? The question that we are asked is, why did the President do it *then*, just when the summit conference that he and the Soviet leadership had labored so hard and so long to arrange was about to occur? The Soviet answer, stilted in form but somehow believable when it is elaborated, is that "it was the will of the people" that the affront be ignored and the summit proceed as promised and planned. The best answer to the Soviet question that I have been able to think up is two-fold. It is that Mr. Nixon cannot tolerate the appearance of defeat in Vietnam, and that he simply reacted in character when he felt that he had been backed into a corner.

When the "will of the people" line was first thrown at me, I dismissed it as the kind of simplistic propaganda to be expected from journalists who are also the servants and spokesmen of their government. But the elaboration of the line, at group receptions and in quiet conversations, convinced me that, along with the propaganda, I was getting some interesting and worthwhile insights into the Soviet regime and Soviet society. At this writing, on the third of Mr. Nixon's eight days in the Soviet Union, when nothing officially told us so far about the summit adds much of value to the knowledge and impressions we brought from Washington, the content and nuances of the informal chitchat seem to me to be more worth reporting than the stuff fed to us in the guise of news. Here, then, is a summary of the impressions that have been derived from conversations with men who are, I am well aware, required by their government and party masters to do what they can to persuade me that the truth is their truth.

The foremost impression is that Leonid Brezhnev, the general secretary of the Communist Party's Central Committee and the Soviet leader with whom Mr. Nixon is principally engaged, is under tremendous pressure to make this conference a real success. It is a pressure that arises from circumstances much more compelling than the Soviet government's specific need for specific agreements on strategic arms limitation, expanded trade with the United States and cooperation in such areas as space exploration, environmental control and public health. The central source of the pressure is fear—the literal fear of nuclear war and nuclear annihilation. One gathers that this fear is infinitely more acute and more alive in the Soviet Union than it has been in the United States since the late 1940s, when Americans as a people seemed to conclude that there was no use worrying about a possibility that appeared to recede with time and familiarity. The possibility and then the announced certainty of a Nixon-Brezhnev summit meeting was received in the Soviet Union as something far more than the prospect of public entertainment, an interesting exercise in big-power diplomacy. It eased the fear. It raised the hope, a hope that became a compelling demand, that nuclear conflict with the United States be removed from the realm of serious possibility.

That accomplished, the fear of nuclear conflict with Communist China would remain, of course. The degree and depth of this apprehension cannot be appreciated in the United States. I have yet to hear it openly and clearly expressed in Moscow. But it is

discernibly present, it is constantly implied in conversations of the
kind upon which I am drawing here. The net effect is to increase,
not diminish, the demand for accommodation with the United
States that presses upon Brezhnev and his fellows in the Soviet
leadership. The thrust, quite explicit and not left to implication, of
conversation on this point is that Brezhnev and the leaders with
whom he had to consult after Nixon delivered his May 8 speech
would never have tolerated the affront to Soviet pride and the
challenge to Soviet policy if they had not been convinced that they
would be inviting serious and possibly unmanageable domestic
trouble for themselves if they canceled the promised summit. The
visitor does not associate unmanageable domestic trouble with this
society and this regime. When I indicated some such thought,
more by a look than in words, one of the Soviet journalists who
had been talking along the foregoing lines said with seemingly
genuine scorn, "Do you believe that our leaders are totally di-
vorced from public sentiment? If you do, you are foolish." Maybe
I was foolish to believe him, but I did.

   The feeling expressed by our Soviet mentors that this meeting
had to occur, that nothing could be allowed to prevent it once it
was agreed upon, is accompanied by a show of profound astonishment and puzzlement. The posed question is not merely why but
how Mr. Nixon could have done what he did on May 8 and
afterward. The idea that any President of the United States could
believe that the American interest in Vietnam and in the outcome
of the Vietnam war is real enough and important enough to justify
the risk to the Moscow summit that Mr. Nixon took is beyond the
ken of the men whose attitudes I am reflecting. In their professed
opinion, it was a very serious risk. They say now, with no evident
sense of contradicting their major point, that they did not see at
the time how Brezhnev and his fellows could avoid cancellation of
the invitation to Nixon, notwithstanding the predictable effect at
home. They doubted then, in short, that Brezhnev and the associated leaders could swallow their own pride and their sense of
national pride and tell Mr. Nixon to come on. One of the editors,
who said that he was sick with fear that the summit would be
canceled, told a family story to make his point that only the most
insistent pressures could have led the leadership to let the confer-

ence proceed. The editor said that his wife and daughter were enraged by the Nixon speech and are still arguing with him that the invitation to Moscow should have been instantly withdrawn. They are not alone in that view, he said, but he thinks Brezhnev and the leaders who sided with him in the decision to go ahead with the conference read the predominant sentiment accurately.

The way in which the journalists whom I am echoing speak of their leaders interests this newcomer to the Moscow scene. They are editors at the second level, sophisticated men, fluent in English, skilled in the arts of persuasion. I doubt that if I were a reporter stationed in Moscow I'd pay them more than the limited and rather casual heed the resident correspondents accord them. One suspects that their knowledge of what goes on at the peaks of Soviet power is at least as modest as that of their professional equivalents among the American correspondents stationed in Washington. But they know enough to perceive, and are brave enough to suggest (with a care for anonymity), that their Brezhnevs and Kosygins are fallible men, capable of error, divided amongst themselves in their secret councils, driven and guided more by circumstance than by ideology. The suggestion is that if this last were not true, Richard Nixon would not be in Moscow, housed in the splendor of the Kremlin Grand Palace and dealing with pragmatists who match him in his readiness to surmount principle when principle gets in the way of desired results. One of the results desired by the President is more Soviet assistance than he has previously obtained in bringing the Hanoi government to the point of productive negotiation in Paris. By productive negotiation, of course, the President means negotiation to end the Indochina war on terms that will leave to him at least a shred of the honor that he keeps talking about. Henry Kissinger, withdrawn from the limelight in Moscow while the President shares it with Brezhnev, didn't bother to equivocate when he was asked to confirm the patent fact that Vietnam is on the summit agenda. In Salzburg, where Nixon paused for a cautionary rest on the way to Moscow, Kissinger said with dry understatement that the Vietnam problem would be discussed but would not overwhelm the occasion. It predictably will not be allowed to do that. But it may be said with confidence that the President will consider his Moscow venture an unalloyed success only if his Soviet hosts are persuaded to do all they can—and that admittedly may not be a great deal—

to convince their ruling friends in Hanoi that Richard Nixon is perfectly willing to leave them in peace with a fair and perhaps better than fair chance to take control of South Vietnam after a decent interval.

Three agreements announced during the first days of the visit solemnized and slightly expanded previously negotiated understandings that the US and the USSR would cooperate in space research and exploration, environmental research and protection, and medical and public health research. The ceremonial signings and the judiciously timed announcements were largely window dressing, designed and arranged beforehand to further the impression that Nixon, Brezhnev and their lesser companions in summitry were accomplishing a lot. But Henry Kissinger had a point when he said in Salzburg that the signing at the summit would have an importance that goes beyond the agreements themselves. It was a demonstration of mutual acceptance of the proposition that agreement to cooperate in a plethora of relatively small matters can hasten progress toward a relationship between the superpowers that diminishes the dangers of conflict over the big issues. The big issue in discussion here, with a hope of concrete and constructive agreement, is strategic arms limitation. That agreement probably will be of sufficient scope to give Brezhnev the appearance of success that he needs in order to justify his submission to Nixon's military measures in Vietnam. If the President has paid a price for the submission, for the permitted summit, and perhaps for Soviet assistance in bringing about a Vietnam settlement that he is capable of accepting, it will be evident when the details of the arms agreement are published and analyzed.

Results aside, the fact that dominates the occasion is that Richard Nixon is here, buddying up with the leaders of the world's greatest Communist power and visibly enjoying his stay in the Kremlin, the cluster of domed temples and palaces and rather shabby office buildings which during most of his career was for him the capital and symbol of detested Communism. The quality of pioneering adventure, of a break from the past that attended his visit to Peking in February is lacking. But the observer must pause at times and succumb to the wonder that this man, this seeming model of mediocrity, should be the first President of the United States to do what he has done this year, within four months, in Peking and now in Moscow.

The people of Moscow pay little attention to his presence. The reporters in Nixon's wake decided that 100,000 people stood along his route from the airport to the Kremlin, but there was no way to count them and many of them appeared to be out for a stroll when the President happened to pass. When he put a wreath on the grave of Moscow's Unknown Soldier, the watching crowd consisted mostly of pedestrians who were forbidden to cross the nearby streets while he was there. Patricia Nixon attracts gangs of the curious when she visits schools, stores, the subway. But Moscow's residents and hordes of tourists from the provinces, reveling in the year's first warm and sunny week, huddle around any person or happening that seems unusual. Four Japanese monks in saffron robes, standing in Red Square before Lenin's tomb, drew a crowd comparable to the ones that Mrs. Nixon draws. One has the impression, though, that this is not indifference and certainly not an ordered show of indifference. On the contrary, the Soviet leaders are using the occasion to invite maximum attention to their association with Nixon. Brezhnev, Kosygin and their fellow dignitaries preen and posture with unmistakable pleasure when they appear with Nixon on Soviet television, signing agreements and toasting with champagne. No doubt about it, the Soviet hierarchy is glad that the President is here and all of us should be too.

June 3, 1972

XVIII

Plus for the President

Warsaw

The wisest thing said by anyone in Richard Nixon's entourage during his eight days at the Moscow summit and his homeward visits to Kiev, Teheran and Warsaw was uttered by Henry Kissinger in a saloon. In order to escape the international hubbub and the complexities of obligatory Russian-English translation at the press center in Moscow, Kissinger turned up once in the American Embassy snack bar and twice in the ghostly twilight of a closed nightclub to explain the mysteries of the summit to reporters who accompanied the President from Washington. The only place available in Kiev for Kissinger's fourth performance was an Intourist bar.

The summit conference had produced a treaty and an interim agreement to limit US and Soviet nuclear armaments, six lesser agreements, a joint communiqué and a statement of "basic principles" which throbbed with peaceful intentions. Some indications that the two governments had got at least a little closer than they had previously been to helping each other bring about a negotiated end of the Indochina war also emerged. The reporters wanted to know whether this orgy of accommodation was ephemeral or whether it really did signal the beginnings of what the communiqué called "a more stable and constructive foundation . . . for the development of peaceful relations and mutually beneficial co-operation between the USA and the USSR." It was midnight. Through a window at Kissinger's back, his questioners could see the lights of the lovely city winking out along both banks of the curving Dnieper River. Kissinger's dumpy figure sagged and his deep voice occasionally shook with fatigue as he leaned on a portable lectern and framed his reply. His answer dealt mostly with the "statement of basic principles," but it was to encompass the whole gamut of summit agreement and discussion. Condensed and slightly tidied up for clarity, here it is:

"We are not naive. It is perfectly possible that six months from now it will turn out that we are again in a period of extreme hostility. If that has happened, both countries will have lost an opportunity and the world will have lost an opportunity. We think the achievement is that we have made these agreements, that SALT has been concluded, and that at least there has been a recognition for the first time on both sides, not just that this or that problem has to be solved but maybe that a new style of international relations has to be developed. How successful we will be in implementing that, only the future will tell. We are not saying that these principles can be a cookbook to which you need merely refer to have a guide for future action. Nor are we saying that it is not perfectly possible that these principles can be broken almost immediately. Nor am I rejecting the possibility at all that they are intended [by the Soviets] as a tactical device to lull certain people. All of this is possible. But if any of these events happen, then we will act with firmness, and some other leaders somewhere along the line will have to address the problem of how to have a peaceful world in an age in which a cataclysm depends on the decisions of men. We have laid out a road map. Will we follow this road? I don't know. Is it automatic? Absolutely not, but it lays down a general rule of conduct through which, if both sides act with wisdom, they perhaps can, over a period of time, make a contribution. At this point it is an aspiration. We would not have signed it [the statement of principles] if we did not believe there was a chance for implementing this aspiration."

The chief American aspirant at the summit, Richard Nixon, buried himself most of the time in the magnificent caverns of the Kremlin Grand Palace, where he and Pat Nixon and Kissinger and a few assistants were quartered. The reporters in his press party

saw more of the President on Soviet television than in the flesh,
and it was not until he left Moscow, after a spectacular farewell
reception for him, that a few stories of how he handled himself
leaked out. Sparse though the accounts were, and designed as they
naturally were to do the President credit, they told something of
him at a peak of hope and effort.

Nixon in Moscow took his penchant for conserving his time
and energies to lengths never before observed by his assistants. In
Washington, a 15-minute appointment might be stretched to 30 or
45 minutes if the subject interested him. In Moscow, his assistants
understood that 15 minutes meant 15 minutes and less if possible.
Mainly preoccupied though he was with summit affairs, he never
loosened his grip on the White House operation at home. Each
day in the Kremlin began with the President's staff chief, H. R.
Haldeman, collecting instructions for telephone relay to George
Shultz and John Ehrlichman at the White House, John Connally
in his last days at the Treasury. They proposed, but Nixon, in
Moscow as in Washington, disposed. Whether in the Kremlin or
aloft in a Soviet Ilyushin-62 enroute to Leningrad and Kiev, his
control of the nuclear command system was as clear and total as it
would have been in Washington.

After Nixon and his principal Soviet host, Leonid Brezhnev,
signed the proposed ABM treaty and the interior offensive arms
agreement late on Friday night in Moscow, the President retired
with Mrs. Nixon and a few assistants from the domed and gold
crusted Vladimir Hall at the Kremlin to the room he used for an
office. There Nixon, Haldeman, Kissinger and others who drifted
in and out talked quietly and shared a modest round of drinks. A
reporter to whom it all seemed mighty restrained on such a great
occasion asked one of the assistants whether the President seemed
to be even mildly elated. "Sure he was," the assistant replied, "but
when he is he doesn't dance a jig, you know."

The President's instructions about Vietnam to Press Secretary
Ronald Ziegler, Communications Director Herbert Klein, and one
or two other assistants who were made available to reporters reflected the extreme sensitivity of the Vietnam issue and Nixon's
desire to discourage speculation to the effect that he had serious
hopes of persuading the Soviet leadership to do what it could to
push the Hanoi leadership toward a more relaxed and amenable
negotiating stance. The instructions were that nothing whatever

was to be said about Vietnam beyond what Nixon and Kissinger had already said—that Vietnam of course had to be and was on the summit agenda—until the summit was over and the agreed official statements were made. I judge from what was said and implied then in the formal statements and by American and Soviet officials that Nixon hopes but still cannot be sure that his Soviet hosts will work quietly with him and Kissinger to persuade the Hanoi government that in the end it may benefit more from a negotiated settlement on terms acceptable to the President than it can from indefinite warfare in South Vietnam with continued American bombing in North Vietnam and continued mining of the entrances to North Vietnam's harbors. Henry Kissinger said at the summit's end, "There were long, sometimes difficult and very detailed discussions on this subject. Whether the two sides understand each other better or whether what they have understood provides the basis for a constructive evolution only the future can say, and I wouldn't want to speculate on that." My impression is that he doesn't want to speculate on it because he awaits a favorable turn in Soviet policy without any Soviet admission that it has occurred, and knows quite well that any official American indication to that effect could wreck whatever prospect there may be of its actually occurring.

The explanations that accompanied publication of the Arms Control Treaty and Interim Agreement were interesting chiefly for their defensive tone and their indication that the President is acutely aware of the vulnerable points. Kissinger, who of course was the principal explainer, labored with all the eloquence and brilliance at his command, along with a dash of sardonic humor, to minimize the vulnerabilities. The essence of his argument, the argument soon to be heard in Congress, was that the continuing nuclear advantage allowed the Soviet Union in offensive missilery, including submarine-launched missiles, if it exercises all of the options permitted by the treaty and the agreement, will at the very worst be less than it would have been without the treaty and agreement at the end of the first five years of negotiated restraint. His overall contention that the great and promising thing is the undertaking of the two major nuclear powers to limit both offensive and defensive nuclear armaments in some degree seemed to me unassailably right.

Throughout the trip, from Moscow to Tehran, the crowds along Nixon's infrequent public routes were curious, passive, never demonstrative. Even at Kiev, a warmer city than Moscow, in the human sense, the thousands who watched him arrive and leave at the inevitable 50-mile-an-hour speeds of Soviet motorcades were so silent that one American reporter called the lively capital of the Ukraine a city of the dead. In Tehran, where the Shah whom Nixon was visiting certainly wanted to show his ally and friend every courtesy, the crowds seldom cheered. Terrorists setting off bombs near a shrine that he visited later, and beside the local USIA building, and a belly dancer climbing onto Henry Kissinger's lap at a press party provided demonstrations of a sort, but not the kind that Nixon laps up. That would come in Warsaw, if at all, and one would have thought that Nixon, busy at the summit though he was, would have spoken occasionally of the enormous welcome that he received here when he came as Eisenhower's Vice President in 1959. Assistants who saw him every day in Moscow said he never mentioned his memory of that visit to them and never suggested that Warsaw had been put on his itinerary in the hope that its people would give him another public triumph on his last stop before flying to Washington. This may have been because his staff and presumably the President didn't know what to expect this time. The Warsaw embassy and the President's advance men reported up to the day he left Tehran that they didn't know whether the Polish government would encourage or discourage a repetition of the frantic 1959 welcome by a quarter-million Poles that led Nixon to call it afterward "a message to free people and to those throughout the world who yearn for freedom, telling them that the torch of freedom still burns in the hearts of millions of Poles despite 14 years of Soviet occupation and Communist rule."

Communist Poland in 1972 was different from the Poland of 1959—a little less repressed, a good deal less subservient to Moscow—and the welcome to Nixon was different. Scores of thousands turned out, and cheered and chanted and sang their pleasure at having Nixon in Warsaw. But, unlike 1959, the authorities were ready for it. Police lining the seven-mile route from the airport into the city prevented the surges into the streets that blocked Nixon's car and overwhelmed the few police on duty then. This time the note was one of friendly curiosity, a sense of

being honored, rather than of protest and yearning. A hundred or
so youngsters, shouting "peace now! peace now!" seemed militant
in a way that most of the cheering, singing, laughing people
around them didn't. An hour after Nixon first passed through the
city's center, the crowds were still out, chanting and singing.
Nixon, holed up with Polish Communist officialdom, must have
thought it a useful prelude to his return and report to Congress on
the Moscow summit.

June 10, 1972

XIX

Selling the Summit

The President was very tired when he ended his Moscow journey with a 10-hour flight from Warsaw, a helicopter jump from Andrews Air Force Base to Capitol Hill, and a televised address to Congress. Steady rain spoiled the rest in the sun that he hoped to get during four days at his Florida home on Key Biscayne. His assistants sensed when he returned to the White House that he still needed calm and time to collect himself for the burst of domestic activity that usually follows his foreign spectaculars and for the quieter job of seeing the defensive ABM treaty and the parallel agreement to limit US and Soviet offensive nuclear arms through Congress.

It appeared during the first week back in Washington that the difficulties with the treaty and agreement would be minimal. Senator Henry M. Jackson did the administration a large favor with his premature complaints of "secret understandings" reached in a "comic opera" atmosphere in Moscow and his hurried charge that the clear advantage in numbers of missile launchers and nuclear submarines allowed the Soviet Union critically endangered US security. Sharp rebukes administered to Jackson on the Senate floor by Mike Mansfield, the Democratic majority leader, and John Sherman Cooper, a respected Kentucky Republican, for attacking the summit results before the treaty and agreement had been submitted to Congress and fully explained, exposed the weakness of the prospective opposition. They also pointed up the strength of the feeling that agreement between the two chief nuclear powers to put some limits on their nuclear armaments, with a joint undertaking to negotiate extension of the first limitations to uncovered weapons and delivery systems, is a great achievement that ought to be obstructed only for the most serious and compelling reasons.

The flabby response to Senator Jackson's talk about "secret understandings" was all the more significant because the President's spokesmen in the Soviet Union, principally Henry Kissinger, had invited precisely that complaint with the only bobble in their initial explanations of the treaty and agreement. Kissinger unaccountably neglected to say on the record, during four expositions of the President's purposes and accomplishment in Moscow, that the written treaty and agreement were supplemented by stipulations which Mr. Nixon made orally to Leonid Brezhnev and Brezhnev made to the President during their discussions. In a huddle with a few reporters after one of his recorded press conferences had ended, Kissinger acknowledged that there were such stipulations and identified one of them. It had to do with the possibility that either the USSR or the US would develop mobile landbased intercontinental launchers, which neither now has, and with them frustrate the satellite detection systems upon which both governments agreed to rely to keep count of each other's nuclear installations. Kissinger said that the President told Brezhnev, and that Brezhnev said he understood, that the US would abrogate the treaty and agreement if it caught the Soviet Union developing mobile land launchers. Mr. Nixon promised before he returned to Washington that summaries of the oral stipulations would be put in writing and submitted to the Senate and House along with the formal documents, and it was upon this promise that Mansfield and Cooper relied when they told Jackson that he was yapping through his hat when he tried to alarm the Senate with his suspicions.

In addition to the aura of acceptance that the President's staff lobbyists detected in Congress, the attitude of one particular senator figured in the assurances conveyed to Mr. Nixon that he can expect easy Senate ratification of the ABM treaty and House-Senate concurrence, invited by him though not legally required,

IF THE PRESIDENT IS STILL INTERESTED IN SUMMITRY....

with the executive agreement to limit offensive arms. The Senator in question is J. William Fulbright, the chairman of the Senate Foreign Relations Committee. Fulbright, embittered by many White House slights and disgusted with Nixon's Vietnam policy, has had few occasions in recent years to support Nixon foreign policy measures with the skill and enthusiasm that he brings to causes he believes in. The word reaching the White House from Senator Fulbright's office is that he is "very, very pleased" with the Moscow results and that he will gladly lead the floor fight for treaty ratification. Fulbright would be less than human, however, if he didn't at least go through the motions of demanding that Henry Kissinger doff his cloak of executive privilege and testify for the treaty and agreement at the committee hearings. After Kissinger's four public appearances before the Nixon press party in the Soviet Union, and with his delayed journey of diplomatic assuagement to Japan in progress while the hearings are being prepared, the President could find it more difficult than it has been in the past to argue that his staff adviser on foreign policy is exempt from formal Senate interrogation. Kissinger said before he left for Japan that he didn't intend to testify, but the expansion of his role as the President's apologist and spokesman has made the continuing claim of executive privacy rather silly.

Some observers of the first arguments for the Moscow arms agreements presented to Congress by the President, Defense Secretary Melvin Laird and Admiral Thomas H. Moorer, chairman of the Joint Chiefs of Staff, thought they spotted an important difference between Mr. Nixon and the Pentagon spokesmen. The President said in his address that he will do everything necessary to sustain US strength and protect US security during the coming period of negotiated nuclear restraint. Laird and Moorer seemed to go beyond this when they told Senate and House subcommittees that the treaty and agreement are acceptable to the defense establishment only if Congress votes requested increases amounting to about $1.8 billion in the pending budget, in appropriations for an advanced strategic bomber, a new generation of nuclear submarines, and development of the multiple targeted warheads and other technological improvements upon which the President depends to maintain effective (though not numerical) parity with the Soviet Union. The difference was illusory. Kissinger, speaking for the President, referred to the same projects when he said in the

Soviet Union that "we will have to continue major programs in those fields in which negotiations are still going forward and in which agreement has not been achieved, because if these negotiations prove anything, it is that it was our unwillingness to disarm unilaterally that has made it possible to get this bilateral agreement."

Buried in this argument was one of the many subordinate features of the Moscow accomplishments that make them true marvels of political skill. No detraction from the President's Moscow success is intended when I note that the performance is tailored to his political needs in this election year. If the argument that the US can bargain safely and effectively with the Soviet Union for nuclear restraint only if it has ample nuclear and other armed might to bargain away is sound, what happens to Senator McGovern's proposal to cut defense appropriations by some $30 billion by 1975? The President has made it hard for McGovern and other advocates of drastic defense reduction to applaud the results of bargaining based, in the official view, upon strength that the cuts would reduce or abolish. Brezhnev and his fellows in the Soviet leadership are invited to Washington—after the 1972 elections. The next phase of strategic arms limitation, the phase intended to level out the Soviet advantage in offensive weapons, is set for negotiation in the fall, when the presidential campaign is on. The commission and consultative bodies established to carry forward US-Soviet trade negotiations, the preliminaries to force reductions in Europe, and a European security conference, are scheduled to get down to serious work and show some results in the same period. All hands are cautioned to wait awhile, conceivably until September or October, for the effects (if any) of the Moscow talks upon negotiations to end the Vietnam war. And there is the Texas Nixocrat, outgoing Treasury Secretary John Connally, sent off to Latin America, Southeast Asia and Europe in a presidential plane to exalt and explain the Moscow achievements, among other things, and get home the day before the Democratic convention opens in Miami Beach. Weary Mr. Nixon, girding himself for the months ahead, has arranged to have a great deal going for him.

June 17, 1972

———

By foolishly knuckling under to Senator Jackson and letting him delay ratification of the ABM treaty for weeks, the Administration complicated and protracted but eventually got the congressional approval of the treaty and the interim agreement on offensive arms. The ongoing negotiations with the Soviet Union proved to be powerful assets for the President during the 1972 reelection campaign.

XX

After the Summits

Here are some judgments, drawn from the public record and set down in advance of the press conference scheduled by the President for June 29, on the results to date of the summit meetings in Peking and Moscow and of Henry Kissinger's return visit to Peking on June 19–23. The record drawn upon is chiefly the one provided by the President at a press conference on June 22 and by Kissinger at four press conferences in the Soviet Union, at another meeting with the press at the White House when he returned from Peking, and at a question-and-answer session with members of Congress on June 15.

My reading of Kissinger's statements in the Soviet Union and in Washington, along with the formal documents issued after the Peking and Moscow summits, is that the President succeeded beyond his hopes in one tremendously important respect and essentially failed in another respect. His success was in bringing the United States, the People's Republic of China and the Soviet Union measurably nearer to that "new international relationship" which he and Kissinger declared to be the primary objective of both summit conferences and of the years of preparation that made them possible. The essence, the indispensable requirement, of that relationship is that each of the super-powers in its dealings with the others give precedence to its own "supreme interests" and to the bearing of those interests upon each other over the interests of the major powers' satellites and dependents. In the terms of greatest current importance to Americans, this means that the United States subordinate its obligation to South Vietnam and its proclaimed interest in a satisfactory outcome of the Vietnam war to its developing relationships with Communist China and the Soviet Union. It also means, of course, that Communist China and the Soviet Union subordinate their obligations to North Vietnam and their interest in an outcome of the Vietnam and Indochina war that would be satisfactory to them to the necessity, now recognized by both Peking and Moscow, for a stable and peaceful relationship with the United States.

Here we come to the President's seeming failure in Peking and Moscow, a failure that has to be defined in relative and extremely uncertain terms. It was to persuade the Peking and Moscow leaderships, principally meaning Mao Tse-tung and Chou En-lai in Peking and Leonid Brezhnev in Moscow, that they have it in their power to persuade if not compel the Hanoi leadership to so alter its bargaining stance in Paris that what Kissinger calls a solution of the Vietnam war "which is just and reasonable for both sides" may at last become negotiable. Kissinger has repeatedly denied that this, stated in these terms, was the President's hope or objective in Peking and Moscow. He has said, and was still saying when he returned from his latest trip to Peking, that the Nixon administration has never asked either the Peking or Moscow governments to "do anything" of the kind. He went so far as to say in Washington on June 24 that "we have no information about the relationship of North Vietnam to its two principal allies."

The denial and the claim do not stand the test of known fact. Before and on May 8, when the President announced the mining of North Vietnam's harbors and the resumption of heavy bombing of North Vietnam, he and Kissinger complained in the plainest and most bitter language that the Soviet Union had made the current Hanoi offensives against South Vietnam possible with its supply of weapons and that the Soviet leaders had misled Kissinger and Nixon into believing that Hanoi's chief negotiator, Le Duc Tho, was ready for productive negotiation with Kissinger. The publication last week of hitherto secret portions of the Pentagon Papers demonstrated that abortive attempts at negotiation in the late 1960s, in which Kissinger was deeply involved for the Johnson administration, rested in part upon a conviction that the Moscow government could assist and was assisting in pressing Hanoi toward useful negotiation. It is believable that Kissinger and Nixon learned from the earlier experience and failure that there are limits to what may be expected of either Peking or Moscow. It is not believable that no effort to renew the attempts occurred at the Nixon summits. Kissinger's frequent refusals to discuss "the substance" of the discussions is just one indication that a great deal that has yet to be published passed between Nixon and his hosts.

It is evident from events that the failure was offset by a very considerable success. The events that make this evident are that Moscow allowed its summit with Nixon to proceed after he announced his determination to do everything in his power to deny Communist China and the Soviet Union further supply access to North Vietnam and that Kissinger was, as he said, "treated with extraordinary courtesy" when he returned to Peking in June. In actions though not in rhetoric, the Peking and Moscow governments have come very close to telling Hanoi that its war is no longer their war. This they have done by tolerating the mining and bombing of North Vietnam and the affront to both the Chinese and Soviet governments that these actions and the Nixon rhetoric that accompanied and still accompanies them constitute. This alone could be—I suspect that it is—the basis for Kissinger's repeated indications at the press conference following his return from Peking that he and the President expect to be in a position to announce that "serious negotiations" with Hanoi are about to be resumed.

A question yet to be answered is the extent, if any, to which the President has subordinated or is prepared to subordinate his interest—he would say, the United States' interest—in the outcome of the Vietnam and Indochina war to the larger relationships that he has labored so long and so hard to develop. The best answer to that question at this writing is another question. Is it conceivable that the Peking and Moscow leaderships would have subordinated their interest in the outcome, to the extent that they have, without a credible indication from the President that he is ready to make some return in kind? A return in kind would have to be a readiness to settle the war on terms short of the ones that he proclaimed on May 8: a return of all American prisoners; "an internationally supervised cease-fire"; a cessation of all American "acts of force" throughout Indochina; the withdrawal within four months of all remaining American forces in South Vietnam; and, at and after that point, "negotiations on a political settlement by the Vietnamese themselves." The President's press secretary, announcing a further reduction of American forces in South Vietnam from 49,000 to 39,000 by September 1, said that the bombing and mining of North Vietnam "are continuing and will continue" until these terms for negotiation are accepted. At Henry Kissinger's post-Peking press conference, however, there were some suggestions of departure from the May 8 terms, and particularly from the undertaking to leave the political settlement to "the Vietnamese themselves."

Kissinger appeared to place total reliance on the bombing and mining and to stand by the latest Nixon terms when he said: "We hope that a further study of the President's May 8th proposal, plus the failure of the [North Vietnamese] offensive to succeed in achieving a military solution for North Vietnam, will convince the leaders of the Democratic Republic to enter serious negotiations." But, in what has to be read as a reference to the Peking and Moscow leaderships, he also said that "we are prepared to listen seriously to the views of others who also have an interest in bringing the war to a conclusion." He remarked that "our efforts over the last weeks" to find a basis for renewed and conclusive negotiation "certainly have not been to bring about a purely military solution." And, in what I took to be his most significant statement, he said: "We expect that when the war is finally settled, it will be through direct negotiations between the North Vietnamese *and American* negotiators." There wasn't one word about leaving the political settlement to "the Vietnamese themselves." This could mean that Richard Nixon intends to be right in there, preventing the imposition of a Communist government upon South Vietnam. My reading of it is that the President hopes and intends to be right in there, during the campaign months of 1972, settling this war on the best terms that he can get and at any necessary cost to his Saigon clients.

July 8, 1972

XXI

Person-to-Person

Laguna Beach, California

The word that seeps from the President's home in San Clemente to the hotel in this resort town where the reporters in his press party are staying, 12 miles up the warm and sunny coast, is that he is in California until mid-July for two principal purposes. One of them is to get the rest that he's needed ever since he made his exhausting trip to Peking four months ago and, according to some of his associates who see him in his private moments, has shown increasing signs of needing since he returned from Moscow. His other purpose, the one with which this report is concerned, is to decide at leisure and away from the pressures of Washington how to conduct his campaign for reelection.

That decision must turn in part upon the nature and outcome of the Democratic convention at Miami Beach. But I have an impression, in the main from interviews in Washington during the fortnight before the President flew to California, that it will largely turn upon Mr. Nixon's appraisal of himself and upon his judgment of how he may best present himself and his first-term record to the country. The required judgment is whether the President himself, Richard Nixon in person, is a more attractive and less repellent figure in 1972 than he knew himself to be in 1968 and found himself to be again in 1970 when he campaigned, with a lack of success that he privately and eventually recognized, for Republican congressional candidates. It is the question and the problem that one of the President's assistants, Patrick Buchanan, had in mind when he told a CBS interviewer the other day that the pre-nomination television effort in 1968 was "structured" to counter the view of "most Republicans" that "Mr. Nixon's personality is not all that good." His judgment as to whether his 1972 personality is "all that good" may be expected to determine the extent to which he stumps the country as candidate Nixon and the extent to which he relies upon his performance as President Nixon to persuade the electorate that he should have a second term.

The assumption at the White House when the President left for California was that his Democratic opponent would be Senator George McGovern. This prospect was taken far more seriously than the national polls and the disarray then evident among the Democrats might have led anyone to assume. The major though not the only reason was that George McGovern is perceived to be a more attractive and credible and decent person than the President is perceived to be. The point is not that the President's assistants and advisers perceive McGovern and Nixon in this way. They do not. The point is the impression, the overwhelming apprehension of the Nixon people, that Sen. McGovern has succeeded and, despite his pre-convention troubles, may continue to succeed in projecting himself to the electorate as the more attractive and credible and decent man of the two. I heard much more talk about the perceived personalities of Richard Nixon and George McGovern than I heard about McGovern's recent maneuvers and equivocation and about the shambles that the Democratic convention could prove to be.

The shorthand truth, not greatly oversimplified, is that the possibility of a head-to-head encounter between Nixon and McGovern, a campaign allowed to be chiefly and basically a contest of personalities, scares some of the President's political advisers and assistants. They are determined not to let it become that kind of campaign and they are praying that the President will agree with them that he might very well lose such a campaign. This is why they are talking up and urging upon him a campaign "on the issues" and, among other things, organizing an enormous research effort, drawing upon all of the informational resources of the federal establishment. It is aimed at demolishing the McGovern position on tax reform, income redistribution, defense cutbacks and the like with Nixon versions of "the facts" instead of relying upon the generalized charge, Agnew-style, that George McGovern is a radical revolutionary engaged in subverting the traditional American verities.

There will be plenty of that sort of rhetoric, capped with the charge that McGovern's advocacy of early and total American withdrawal from Indochina amounts to a call for shameful surrender. In quarters near the President, however, the inquirer detects a suspicion that this line of talk about and against Sen. McGovern won't wash. One of the President's political pragmatists, Harry Dent, has seen some samples of McGovern's TV spots and has reported that the candidate who comes across from them conveys to the viewer a conviction of simple honesty and sincerity that has little if anything to do with the declared McGovern positions, including those thought at the White House to be most vulnerable to gut attack. There is a feeling, a genuine and expressed fear, that attempts to impugn McGovern's integrity and loyalty will or would serve to magnify his personal appeal and assist him in promoting the impression that he is a fundamentally decent man who is up against a fundamentally indecent opponent. A related feeling, not expressed in so many words but clearly implied, is that the President will do himself a grave and perhaps disastrous disservice if he succumbs once more, as he did in 1970, to his inclination to go for the jugular and thereby emphasizes the perceived contrast between him and McGovern. A politician in White House employ who professes to be quite sure that Mr. Nixon has no such intention thinks it nonetheless in order to say, "it would be a great mistake, the way to defeat."

The assumption, just short of certainty, that Mr. Nixon currently intends to keep Spiro Agnew on the ticket is a cause for unease tempered by the further assumption that the Vice President's savage tendencies can and will be brought under adequate White House control. A study of the speeches the Vice President has been delivering since April suggests that this may not be as difficult as his critics are likely to suppose. Along with Agnew's customary scatter-gun invective, there is a heavy injection of researched fact (or alleged fact) that may be read to indicate that he is adjusting himself to the prospect of a judiciously restrained campaign "on the issues."

A cause for comfort at the White House is the abrupt departure of John Mitchell from the Committee for Reelection of the President and his replacement by Clark MacGregor, a former Minnesota congressman who has been on the White House staff since early 1971. MacGregor's assets include the fact that he is accustomed to taking orders from the two White House assistants, H. R. Haldeman and John Ehrlichman, to whom lesser Nixon minions look for political direction. During his brief tenure at the committee, after he ceased to be attorney general, Mitchell worked and consulted more closely with Haldeman and Ehrlichman—particularly with Haldeman—than was generally realized. But his high standing with the President, his equally high estimation of himself, and his stature as a former Cabinet officer precluded the degree of direct White House control of the developing campaign that a good many people around Mr. Nixon anticipate and believe to be necessary. The satisfaction over Mitchell's departure implies no doubt that he quit because and only because he said he did, for the sake of his family and at the insistence of his troubled wife, Martha Mitchell. I hear and am disposed to believe that the satisfaction goes all the way up to the President. Mr. Nixon, acknowledging that mistakes were made in the 1970 campaign for congressional supporters, has said that when it's his campaign, he runs it. Now he's free to do so.

July 15, 1972

How, when this was written, I could have ignored the arrest on June 17 of five electronic buggers in the Watergate headquarters of the Democratic National Committee baffles me in early 1973. Put it down to my reluctance to believe the possible worst about Richard Nixon.

XXII

A Private Affair

San Clemente, Calif.

On the second Sunday of the President's midsummer stay in California, he and Mrs. Nixon visited four members of her family—two brothers, a half-brother, and a sister—at the half-brother's home in Las Feliz, a moderately affluent section of Los Angeles. It was a minor occasion, hardly worth the little attention it got. The Nixons were at the home of their host, Matthew Bender, for 93 minutes, and were back at their seaside estate and the adjoining Western White House on the outskirts of San Clemente three hours after they left by helicopter. The trip is reported here because certain events that occurred in connection with it illustrate the rigor with which Richard Nixon tries to enforce his view that he is entitled to privacy when he wants it and is equally entitled to maximum public exposure in the fashion and only in the fashion he desires when that is what he wants.

The jaunt to Los Angeles was in the category that the White House staff calls "movements." The term sometimes heard is "those goddamned movements." Movements differ in several ways from full-scale presidential journeys. In contrast to the elaborate planning, the fleets of official and chartered jets, the crowds and motorcades and swarms of journalists that the trips from city to city and country to country entail, movements are brief and sudden forays, often undertaken on whim, from wherever the President is lodged to a golf course, a beach, a favorite restaurant, a church, or to nowhere in particular on drives through the countryside. They occur in Washington, but the President has more leisure for them and they are easier (though never easy) to arrange when he is at his homes in California and Florida.

One of the differences between movements and journeys has to do with the press and the President's ambivalent attitude toward it. The reporters, cameramen and technicians who accompany the President on the organized trips do so (or think they do) as a matter of right. Within very few limits, they are free to report all that he says and photograph and film all that he does in public, and the White House has no control over the use of the reports and pictures. The White House press corps vehemently asserts a right but really has no right, at any rate no recognized right, to accompany the President on his movements. In this and previous regimes, dating back at least to Franklin Roosevelt's, there have been understandings between the press and Presidents that the incumbent will let a small "pool" of reporters and cameramen tag along with him and stay somewhere near him, though not always in direct sight of him. John Kennedy and Lyndon Johnson were notorious for breaching the understandings that prevailed in their time and Nixon did it twice during the first ten days of his current stay in California, once to slip away to a beach near his home and again to dine with a couple of chums at a nearby restaurant.

For three discernible reasons, however, he has been fairly good about it. The first reason is that he knows as well as the journalists do why these restricted groups are called protective pools. They are along in case "something happens" to the President, the something most in the minds of all concerned being what happened to President Kennedy and could have happened—the possibility is never far from the thoughts of anyone around the White House—to Richard Nixon during his family visit to Los Angeles. The second reason is that it's a pretty safe procedure for this or any President. Because the poolers, particularly the cameramen, are present on sufferance, they are under effective White House control. If the President or his press spokesman tells the reporters that an entire movement or any part of it is off the record, it stays off

WHY THE PRESS DOESN'T HAVE DICK NIXON TO KICK AROUND ANYMORE

the record. If the rule is "no pictures," there won't be any pictures for print or television. The third reason is that Mr. Nixon never knows when he will want reporters and cameramen at hand to publicize some unexpected event—a chance encounter with a friendly crowd, for instance—that may serve him well in print or on television. No President in memory has resented the insistent watching eye of the media more than he does, and none has valued media presence at useful moments more than he does.

Protective pools invariably include two reporters and two photographers representing AP and UPI. A third reporter for a newspaper or news magazine is usually included. The signal that the President expects something good to turn up during a movement is the presence of a silent-film cameraman. If a technician required for television sound film is along, the assumption is that there's going to be lots of reportable action. The pool chosen by the White House press staff for the Los Angeles trip included the usual three reporters and two wire-service photographers, plus an ABC network film man and an audio technician. A White House staff photographer and a White House audio technician were also assigned. All of them were called to duty on half an hour's notice, indicating that the President had decided only that morning to accompany Mrs. Nixon. Subsequent events indicated that he may not have had or taken time to tell his assistants what he expected and wanted and that they, knowing from experience that Richard Nixon becomes very temperish indeed when his demands for media coverage are not instantly and amply met, expanded the pool beyond the customary size in order to forestall any possible trouble.

The helicopter pad at the Western White House has plenty of room for two choppers, and the poolers hoped to be taken there so that they could watch the Nixons and their staff party board the President's helicopter and take off. The poolers were sent instead to an auxiliary pad, well away from the Nixon compound. Aboard the chopper assigned to them, they were allowed to hover above the President and his party while they embarked. The pool chopper returned to the auxiliary pad, picked up six Secret Service agents and flew ahead of the President's helicopter to a public-school playground near the home of Mrs. Nixon's half-brother,

Matthew Bender. Robert Hemmig, the network cameraman, mindful that a President's helicopter can crash, turned his camera on the Nixon craft and filmed its approach and landing. The AP and UPI photographers took no pictures, then or later. Hemmig's camera was still running when Mrs. Nixon, followed by the President, emerged from their helicopter and walked toward the poolers. Stephen Bull, a Nixon assistant, and a military aide, marine Major Jack Brennan, saw what Hemmig was doing and rushed toward him, signaling "no pictures" with forefingers sawing across their throats. A Secret Service agent ran up to Hemmig, shouting "no pictures." Hemmig immediately stopped his camera. Jack D'Arcy, a young press officer who assembles and shepherds the movement pools, told Hemmig after the party arrived at the Bender home, in cars driven up from San Clemente to Los Angeles, that he had to make sure that the film was never used. Without argument and after some friendly discussion, Hemmig removed the film and gave it to D'Arcy. D'Arcy threw it into one of the pool cars and said later that he supposed it had been destroyed. While the poolers and a bevy of Secret Service agents stood outside the Bender home, the White House photographer was called inside to take pictures of the President with his wife and her relatives. Except for Matthew Bender, who was ill, the group walked out to the front porch at the end of the visit and stood there a while, chatting and saying goodbye. The reporters and photographers in the street said that it was a pleasant and warming scene, the kind they'd have thought the President would want to be seen in print and on the tube. But the order was still "no pictures," local photographers and cameramen were barred from the street by the Secret Service, and no pictures were taken. At the school grounds, when the party returned, many of some 200 people standing near had cameras and were shooting away, but no news pictures were permitted then, either. Back at San Clemente, the press chopper again hovered above the President and his companions while they debarked. The poolers then landed at the auxiliary pad, with nothing to show and nothing much to report except that the President evidently wanted the trip with his wife to see her relatives to be considered a private affair.

July 22, 1972

———

Quite unjustly, after reading this report, Hemmig's superiors at ABC rebuked him for giving in to D'Arcy, and Press Secretary Ronald Ziegler rebuked D'Arcy for talking to me.

XXIII

Agnew Again

The President could have made a big show of announcing that he had decided to keep Vice President Agnew on the 1972 ticket. He didn't and here is a guess, derived from conversations at the White House, at why he didn't. Spiro T. Agnew in 1972 is a known figure, variously admired and detested, judged by some to be fit and by others unfit for his present office and for the highest office, in a way that he was not known and appraised in 1968. Mr. Nixon was 56 when he was inaugurated in 1969; he will be 60 when and if he is inaugurated in 1973. Many more people will be thinking in 1972 than were thinking in 1968 that in voting for Nixon-Agnew they will be voting for a Vice President who at any moment could become President Agnew. They will be wrestling with the thought that Senator George McGovern, the Democratic nominee, drily expressed at the end of a CBS television interview on July 23 when he said the announcement "does give us some indication as to the kind of man the President wants to run this country."

Mr. Nixon cannot drive the thought from the electoral mind. He cannot eliminate and he can do very little to diminish the hazards of mortality. But he can do a good deal to minimize and mitigate the effects that the thought and the hazards may have upon his own candidacy. In particular, he can minimize and discourage the assumption that in retaining the Vice President on the

Republican ticket this year he is setting up Mr. Agnew for the Republican nomination for the Presidency in 1976. He has kept the Vice President at a distance throughout the first term, demonstrating that his Vice President doesn't have to be his man in the sense of one who is entitled to regular and intimate association and consultation. This process of deliberate disassociation was taken to the extreme in recent months, when the President dangled his Texas Nixocrat, John B. Connally, before Agnew and the country as a possible alternative for this year's ticket and refused to discuss the matter with the Vice President. The hour that Nixon and Agnew spent together in the Oval Office on July 21, giving and getting the word at last, was the first such occasion in a long while. Agnew barely suggested the intensity and depths of the frustration and pain he had endured in the past months of demeaning uncertainty when he said after the decision was announced, "I guess everybody has moments of insecurity from time to time, but I never did really feel that I was in deep trouble, you might say, as far as the selection was concerned." So proud a man must have suffered, even in the moment of declaring his pleasure at being selected, when a reporter asked him what he said to the President and he answered: "I simply said, 'Mr. President, I am delighted to have the chance to serve again with you, and I will do everything I can to see that we are reelected.' "

The way in which the President made the smallest possible show of the announcement is worth recording. He returned from a fortnight in California on Tuesday, spent the working week in hot and smoggy Washington, and called Agnew into the Oval Office at the White House on Friday afternoon. As he has done for much less important announcements, he could then have appeared with Agnew in the White House press room, before TV cameras and a crowd of byline writers. Instead he helicoptered to Camp David, the presidential haven in the nearby Maryland mountains, for dinner with John Connally. He returned briefly to Washington on Saturday, not to announce anything but to attend the wedding of a friend of his daughter, Julie Eisenhower. Earlier on Saturday, usually an empty day for the media at the White House, reporters were given an hour's notice that Press Secretary Ronald Ziegler would hold a briefing "for sound and film." Ziegler announced, in the flattest conceivable fashion, that the President had informed various Republican dignitaries "of his intention to recommend to the Republican National Convention the nomination of Vice President Agnew for a second term. As President Nixon said in January, in an interview [with Dan Rather of CBS], he believes that you should not break up a winning combination." Apart from the names of the Republicans who'd been told about it and the fact that the President "informed the Vice President of his decision" at the Friday afternoon meeting, that was it. Ziegler said that reporters who wanted to hear from Agnew could do so if they went out to Andrews Air Force Base, a longish drive from Washington, where the Vice President would be having a press conference before he took off for the West Coast and Alaska. The press secretary also did what he could, short of meeting the question directly, to discourage the instant speculation that the President was having his decision announced then, somewhat earlier than his political assistants had expected it, in order to shut off a rising and potentially embarrassing "stop Agnew" movement among such Republicans as Senators Jacob Javits of New York and William Saxbe of Ohio. A few newspaper and magazine editorialists were demanding that Agnew be dumped, and conservative Nixon supporters were threatening to desert the ticket if he was. "Actually," Ziegler said, "it comes down to this. The President had made his decision and, therefore, wanted to announce it."

A lot of private White House activity preceded the announcement. H. R. Haldeman, John Ehrlichman and Charles Colson, the three Nixon assistants most involved in seeing to it that campaign attitudes and tactics are shaped up in the way the President wants them shaped, have recently had some earnest and friendly conversations with the Vice President. Much as the fact may surprise people who think of Haldeman and Colson as perhaps the toughest hard-liners in the President's immediate service, the thrust of their talks with Agnew was that the Vice President, for his own and the President's good, has got to cool down without entirely abandoning his attacks on media liberals, negative elitists, and the whole spectrum of anti-Nixon types who somehow get identified as traitorous revolutionaries in the familiar Agnew rhetoric. Agnew speeches in Oregon, Alaska, and Spokane, Wash., during the first tour he made after he was reanointed by the President, reflected either the White House advice or (as is quite believable) his own judgment of the tone he should strike in the 1972 campaign. The speeches were (for him) moderate, conciliatory and, as he has mournfully predicted such speeches would be, not very quotable. The worst he had to say about the environmentalists who oppose the horrifyingly destructive trans-Alaska oil pipeline was that they are "anti-progress." His discussion in Portland, at a gathering of small-town editors, of the relationship between government and the media was a model of intelligent restraint. He actually said, "The substance of my remarks, then, is that we all, whether government official or editor, might do well to forego harangue and cliché in favor of discussion based on reason and public interest." Among others at the White House, Bob Haldeman let it be known at the end of the Agnew tour that he was pleased with the Vice President's performance. One may suspect that Haldeman was also surprised, relieved, and keeping his fingers crossed.

Whether to leave Agnew to his own staff and devices or to surround him with a crew of Nixon assistants, as was done for the 1970 mid-term campaign, was a question discussed but not decided during the week preceding the President's proxy announcement. The Vice President resented the implication in 1970 that the President thought him incapable of conducting a satisfactory mid-term campaign without White House oversight, and the assignment of four Nixon assistants to Agnew saddled the President with indisputable responsibility for the abrasive assaults and tactics that in the outcome proved to be more damaging than helpful. Patrick Buchanan, one of two Nixon speech-writers assigned to Agnew in 1970, has heard unofficial speculation that he may get the same chore this year, but at this writing nobody at the White House has discussed the possibility with him. Bryce Harlow, the assistant who headed the Agnew team in 1970, is no longer at the White House and no assistant there now has Agnew's confidence to the extent that Harlow had it. There will be a watch on Agnew, that's for sure. How to mount and keep it is a nice question, the kind that President Nixon terms "a close call," and it probably won't be decided before he and his Vice President are renominated in August.

August 5 and 12, 1972

For an account of Agnew campaigning under remote control, see page 146.

XXIV

The Loved One

At this writing, ten days before the Republicans assemble in Miami Beach to renominate the President and Vice President, a feeling that is new to the Nixon White House is apparent all over the place. It is a feeling, expressed in tones of muted astonishment, that millions of somebodies out there actually like Richard Nixon. The opposite impression that most people, including a distressing proportion of those who voted for him in 1968 and are counted upon to vote for him this year, don't really like him has dominated and darkened the atmosphere of the White House since Mr. Nixon occupied it in 1969. His examinations of himself, in speeches and interviews and a book, have been studded with awareness that he has been widely disliked as a person. He said in 1968 that he didn't expect to be liked and hoped only to be respected in the presidency. Until recently, very few Nixon assistants would have quarreled in their honest moments with George McGovern's remark to columnist Mary McGrory that "I don't think the country likes that guy." A sense that this was all too true lay behind the frequent advice to him that he hold his personal campaigning to a minimum and postpone the minimum to the last weeks of the 1972 campaign. Now all that is changing, partly because the apprehension has lessened and partly because the

President is resisting the advice and indicating a desire to take early to the stump and press the electoral flesh soon and often.

Just what has brought about the change is hard to fathom. The national polls, including one that appeared to reflect a high level of trust in him as a person and a President, have something to do with it but don't wholly explain it. Such staff operatives as Harry Dent, the President's southern specialist, tell him that they find in their visitations around the country a positive liking not only for his policies but for him, and that sort of reporting from men who have trained themselves to guard against over-confidence and to discount the fact that they are usually in touch with committed supporters must have a certain effect. But I attribute the change chiefly to two other factors, both of which can be appreciated only if the paranoia that has marked the Nixon White House is adequately understood and appreciated.

The first factor, directly connected with that paranoia, is the phenomenal success of the staff effort to protect the President from personal involvement in and responsibility for incidents and situations that could have and, I strongly suspect, should have made the perceived rise in personal liking for and confidence in him impossible. The classic instance is the International Telephone and Telegraph scandal that never became a presidential scandal. It involved, remember, an administratively imposed antitrust settlement that was costly to ITT but could have been far worse for it, and ITT's undertaking to guarantee part of the costs of the aborted plan—Mr. Nixon's plan—to hold the Republican convention in San Diego. Attorney General John N. Mitchell, by the President's account his most valued Cabinet associate and adviser until John Connally came along, got away with his denials of substantial participation in the settlement and knowledge of the convention commitment. Richard Kleindienst, the successor at Justice, was hurt, but not enough to deny him the office the President conferred upon him. Peter Flanigan, a senior White House assistant, admitted to a modest part in the antitrust settlement but never had to acknowledge that he so much as discussed it with the President. William Timmons, the Nixon assistant charged with overseeing the San Diego arrangements, was seldom mentioned in the news accounts of that aspect of the affair. This remarkable exercise in presidential protection could be put down to the normal functions of any President's staff. But, for reasons connected

THE SENATE JUDICIARY HEARINGS GET CURIOUSER AND CURIOUSER

with the second factor—the paranoiac Nixon view of the national
media—it went beyond the norm.

The extreme effort to protect Mr. Nixon arose from a conviction that the national media, printed and electronic, would savage
this President with singular and deliberate ferocity if he were personally hooked up in the slightest factual degree with either the
antitrust or the San Diego arrangements. A former Nixon assistant, James Keogh, made a book (*President Nixon and the Press*)
out of the related certainties that most national journalists dislike
Nixon as a man and are moved by liberal bias to misrepresent and
mistreat him as they would never abuse one of Spiro Agnew's
liberal elitist "radiclibs" in the same office. Coming to the current
point, some of the most serious preparations for Mr. Nixon's 1972
campaign were founded on the assumption that the national media
would be kind to and biased toward any of the prospective Democratic nominees, and especially toward George McGovern once he
became the expected nominee, in ways that the press would never
be kind to Richard Nixon. The thought that a significant number
of national reporters, columnists and broadcasters could be posi-
tively unkind to a George McGovern was utterly beyond the belief
and comprehension of most of the Nixon staff until McGovern got
into his vice presidential trouble. [A reference to the choice and
dumping of Senator Thomas Eagleton as Senator McGovern's vice-
presidential running mate, a situation that was not reported in
these columns.—J.O.]

The resultant coverage and comment, on the whole more acrid
and searching and destructive than any experienced by the President since he took office, had a mixed and rather weird effect at
the White House. The unbelievable had to be believed and welcomed; the impossible was proven possible. Some of the hardened
paranoiacs (H. R. Haldeman and Charles Colson come to mind)
were said to argue that it was a passing aberration, one that the
deviant journalists would soon correct, but at the moment unre-
constructed cynics appear to be in the minority. A decision to
moderate the Vice President's and others' attacks upon the basic
credibility of the media predated the McGovern troubles and coverage. It arose from a simpler realization that this particular part
of the general plan, still in force and being intensified, to brand
Nixon critics as irresponsible and dangerous radicals hadn't paid
in the past and was unlikely to pay in 1972. The effect of the

recent McGovern coverage upon the Nixon entourage was more subtle. The immediate effect was to make ridiculous the paranoiac illusion that this President is uniquely exposed and vulnerable to critical coverage and comment and to impair the companion illusion that the country's most influential journalists and commentators are determined to see that he is never liked because they don't like him and his policies.

In ways that may be sensed around the White House but cannot be documented, the end effect has been to make believable, to an extent it previously wasn't, the astounding impression that the President has come to be liked as a person by significant numbers of people and voters who might prefer him to an opponent but—it had been supposed—could never like him.

All of which is not to suggest that the protective operation has been abandoned or modified. It is presently directed at keeping the President immune from any suggestion or provable showing that he had anything to do with the bugging of the Democratic National Committee's headquarters in Washington. One of the five buggers (or de-buggers) caught in the act was a security officer and consultant for both the Republican National Committee and the campaign adjunct of the White House, the Committee for the Reelection of the President, when he and the others were arrested on June 17. A check for $25,000 in consolidated campaign contributions somehow got from former Secretary of Commerce Maurice Stans, the President's chief fund-raiser, to the Miami bank account of one of the arrested buggers. Attendant circumstances, too complex for detailing here, have compelled a Nixon assistant, Charles Colson, literally to raise his right hand and swear to at least three staff associates that he had nothing to do with it. The President has assigned another assistant, John Dean, to follow and oversee the efforts of the FBI and the local federal prosecutor in Washington to identify the person or persons who ordered the bugging. White House reporters keep needling Press Secretary Ziegler about Colson, but I have yet to hear Dean mentioned at a Ziegler briefing as the one man around the President who is bound to know the facts if anybody does. The hope at the White House is that the ultimate responsibility will be brought no nearer to the President than some mid-level nitwit at the reelection committee. The consuming dread in Mr. Nixon's vicinity is that somebody will recall a casual remark by him to the effect that it would be nice to know what was going on at the Democratic headquarters. He never said this, so far as I know. But eager beavers have picked up and acted upon equivalent remarks, with unhappy consequences. It's the sort of thing that could reverse the President's supposed rise in public liking and personal esteem.

August 19 and 26, 1972

After the foregoing report appeared, I was told at the White House that the reference to recollection of "a casual remark" by the President got closer to the prevailing apprehensions than he and his people wanted any reporter to get.

XXV

Beach Party for
the President

Miami Beach

This report on the promotional fantasy that the President and his imagists chose to make of the Republican convention begins with a little advice to people who think of themselves as liberals and have a gut belief that the country should be able to do better for itself than it will if it gives Richard Nixon another four years in the White House.

The advice is to take the fantasy and the Republicans who played their appointed parts in it very seriously indeed. A reporter could not be here through the week of public and secret committee work that preceded the convention without perceiving that these are serious people, seriously engaged in preparing the way to the victory that they expect in November and intent upon using the victory to consolidate Republican power for years to come over a nation molded and accustomed to a Republican pattern of minimal and orderly change. There is a reality behind the projected fantasy, a strength in these happy products and beneficiaries of an ordered society, that must be recognized and respected if the advocates of a more open and relaxed and generous society who put their hopes in George McGovern are to have the slightest chance of prevailing. Senator McGovern is trying to provoke a contest of

personalities, on the assumption that he attracts and Nixon repels
enough voters to decide the outcome. The President and his advisers have been afraid, but are less afraid now than they were a
few weeks ago, that it could be turned into just that kind of
contest. The damage that Senator McGovern has done to himself,
at least temporarily, and a conviction that the marvelous chemis-
try of the presidency has transformed Nixon from a repellent into
an attractive personality, have persuaded some of his advisers and
seem to have persuaded him that the kind of contest they recently
dreaded would be to his advantage and to his opponent's disad-
vantage. Ten days with the President's Republicans in Miami
Beach have persuaded me that it's a secondary question, at best.
The question that matters, the question the voters will be answering in November, is whether enough of them to give Mr. Nixon
the anticipated victory see in his Republicans at Miami Beach and
in the life and society that they personify the life and society that
most Americans want for themselves.

The Republicans at the Miami Beach convention were mostly
white, mostly well-off, mostly in or near middle age, mostly male.
Fifty-six of the 1348 delegates and 84 of the 1348 alternate delegates were black. Women were in the minority, though the largest
minority they have ever managed to muster at a Republican convention. These familiar statistics barely suggest the essential point,
which is that the Republican Party mirrored at this convention is
predominantly determined to preserve the character and the attitudes and the balance of demographic and regional power that
produced the 1972 proportions. The party wants more young voters, more blacks and minority "ethnics." It did more at this convention to attract them with changes in structure and rules than
the boldest advocates of change expected it to do. But what it
refused to do was more indicative of the party's fundamental nature than what it did.

It refused to require state and local party organs to do anything
whatever to draw the wanted young, blacks and women into the
fold and further refused to require that they be sent in enlarged
proportions to the 1976 convention. One of the declared reasons
for declining to go beyond encouragement to mandatory requirement was at once spurious and a testament to the ability of otherwise rational people to deceive themselves. The argument that
invariably quelled the calls in the pre-convention committee meet-

ings for direct and drastic change was that the McGovern Democrats had taken the mandatory route and look what they had done
to the Democratic Party and to its July convention in the same
hall at Miami Beach. The myth that the Democratic convention
was a chaotic disaster, rather than the orderly proceeding that it
actually was, figured prominently and frequently in the Republican debate. The other reasons advanced were more cogent and
harder to question on factual grounds. Mandatory requirements
meant quotas, and quotas were acknowledged by the most insistent proponents of an open and broadened party to be bad in
principle and awkward in practice. Explicit requirements, however
carefully they might be phrased to minimize or evade the quota
stigma, would invite a plethora of credentials disputes and, what
was worse, would stimulate litigation and judicial intervention of
the sort that was already plaguing the party. All of these arguments, genuine and spurious, were highly convenient to the dominant Republicans who want to keep the party pretty much as it is,
with a premium on disciplined order and, so they suppose, a growing appeal to voters who are presumed to want the same quality in
their society and their lives.

This desire and this appraisal of the public mood conditioned
everything that the convention and its preparatory committees did
in Miami Beach. The fantasy devised by the President's professional promotionists and presented on television was designed to
exaggerate the degree of order and unity that actually exists within
the party and to contrast the conveyed impression with the potential for disorder that is associated in Nixon propaganda with
George McGovern and his Democrats. Adding up the factors that
assist the President and his publicists in this endeavor is a fascinating exercise. Among the factors are the waverings and contra-
dictions that have appeared, or been made to appear, to mar the
performance of Senator McGovern since he was nominated. His
contribution to the Nixon strategy in this respect has been substantial enough to arouse an odd worry. Over morning coffee on
the second day of the convention, a Nixon assistant remarked with
a distinctly unconvincing laugh that he was beginning to wish the
news media would pay less attention than they had been paying to
the senator's slips and troubles. He discerned a danger, the assistant said, that the anticipated victory would be adjudged a Mc-
Govern disaster rather than a Nixon triumph.

No such reservation diminished the pleasure with which the Nixon people contemplated the anti-Nixon and antiwar street protests. The obstructions of traffic and access to the convention hall, the burning of pot and flags, the trashing of a hotel lobby and the abuse, verbal and physical, aimed at delegates heightened the contrast between the forces of order and the forces of disorder that the campaign tacticians wanted to make. The tragedy for the country, though not for the Nixon people, was that the miscellaneous yippies, fags, dykes and extreme militants who monopolized the news during the first days of the convention obscured the steady discipline of the Vietnam Veterans Against the War and the main forces of dissent assembled by David Dellinger and Rennie Davis in the Miami Conventions Coalition. Watching the unkempt legions of the outraged and in some instances outrageous young at their work in the streets, I concluded that they were driven to excess by a sense of their own futility. I was torn between admiration for the best of them and regret that they were so effectively assisting the Nixon design.

The sole issue that caused a ruckus on the convention floor got there only because the party was under the pressure of a suit brought by the Ripon Society, a tiny organization of liberal and mostly young Republicans. A federal judge in the District of Columbia upheld the society's contention that the method of apportioning national convention delegates among the states was unconstitutionally arbitrary and forbade the 1972 convention to apply it to the 1976 convention. The overturned rule was heavily weighted in favor of small states and against the big states; it was especially dear to southern and some western Republicans. The effort of big-state liberals to seize the advantage from small-state conservatives and confer it upon themselves with a new rule raised a tremendous storm in two convention committees, the Republican National Committee and finally on the convention floor. The end results were a sound defeat for the liberals and a revised rule, also of doubtful constitutionality, which increases the total number of delegates and the size of 48 state delegations but leaves the smaller states with just about the proportionate weight they previously enjoyed. One of the few laughable features of this thoroughly honed convention was the solemnly asserted claim of the liberal and conservative antagonists that it wasn't a fight between them for control of the 1976 convention. It was precisely that. A victory for the liberals could have doomed whatever chance Vice President Spiro Agnew may have for elevation to the presidency and improved the rather dim prospects of Senator Charles Percy of Illinois, who was accused in committee of supporting the liberal position for that reason. The White House claim that the numerous Nixon assistants who were in Miami Beach before and throughout the convention stayed out of the apportionment struggle was false. Nixon men put together the basic elements of the amendment that was finally adopted, and others followed the complex committee proceedings like sparrows fluttering over an imperiled fledgling.

The major and most obvious White House oversight was reserved for the party platform. It is loaded with misplaced cracks at George McGovern, the hard tone of the references to the Vietnam war would give me chills if I attached much importance to them, and the harsh anti-busing plank reflects Nixon at his vote-hunting worst. But, considering that it is in essence a Nixon production, the document on the whole could be a lot worse than it is. I take most of the hard-line planks to be concessions to party conservatives that need not debar the President from choosing a different course in the second term if he is so inclined. I have a hunch that on many domestic issues (busing excluded) he will be so inclined if he is reelected.

The resident honcho for domestic purposes in Miami Beach was John D. Ehrlichman, the assistant for domestic affairs. A White House man said of Ehrlichman's convention role, "John is the gentleman with the feather-light touch on the lady's arm, guiding her across the street." Two of his assistants, Edward Harper and Edward L. Morgan, were in regular communication with the platform committee staff. The absent but supreme honcho was H. R. Haldeman, who spent the pre-convention week at Camp David, near Washington, with the President. Assistants in Miami Beach consulted him by telephone on critical problems. Reaching him was difficult at times and when it was the decisions were either delayed or evaded. Henry Kissinger, who accompanied the President to Miami and happily preened for TV cameras within minutes of his first arrival at the convention hall, was represented during the pre-convention week by one of his NSC assistants, John Lehman. Lehman and Ehrlichman were involved in the two most direct and explicit White House interventions in the final platform process. One of the interventions was the only instance in which the platform committee was flatly told that the President wanted certain language and would accept no other language. It concerned a foreign policy plank (I don't know which one); there was a fierce fight within the committee, and the President's language was accepted.

The other direct intervention concerned the labor plank. Ehrlichman telephoned Representative John Rhodes of Arizona, the touchy and independent committee chairman, and said he was relaying a message straight from the President. The message was that the President wanted a labor plank that would be thoroughly acceptable to organized labor. The references in the 1968 platform to the Taft-Hartley Act and its hated section 14-B, which authorizes government intervention in emergency strikes, were to be dropped entirely, and above all there must not be the slightest intimation that the Republican Party and the administration favor right-to-work laws which bar the closed shop. Rhodes never mentioned this conversation to the full committee, but other members relayed the President's wishes with such assurance that all present understood that they were getting the White House word. Again there was a fierce fight, and again the President prevailed. Proof that AFL-CIO President George Meany was pleased, as the President intended him to be, came when Treasury Secretary George Shultz, an old hand at labor dealings, flew to Washington for a golf game with Meany and returned to Miami Beach the following day. Meany had invited Shultz to be his partner in a tournament sponsored by Meany.

The chief platform writers were Bryce N. Harlow and Martin Anderson. Harlow was a Nixon assistant with cabinet rank during the first two years of the first term. As White House and congressional staff man, he has worked on every Republican platform since 1956. When not in government employ, he has been Procter and Gamble's chief Washington lobbyist for many years. Anderson, also a former Nixon assistant, is still an intermittent White House consultant on per diem pay. He is a senior fellow of the Hoover Institution at Stanford University. Since he went to work on the platform for Rhodes last April, he has been on leave and the Republican National Committee payroll. When a reporter

asked Rhodes whether it was proper for a corporate lobbyist to be
writing a party platform, the chairman gave the impression that
Harlow was on his staff and added, "When he works for me, he
works for me and not for anybody else." This was not technically
true, though anyone who knows Bryce Harlow would suppose that
it was true in spirit. Harlow continued to be paid by Procter and
Gamble during his work for Rhodes in Washington and Miami
Beach. I am told and believe that a newspaper report that Harlow
blocked a plank advocating a tighter lobby registration law is in
error. The plank died in a subcommittee with which Harlow had
no connection.

Representative Paul McCloskey of California, who briefly ran
against Nixon for the presidential nomination in order to drama-
tize opposition to the Vietnam war, gave two antiwar veterans
guest tickets to the convention hall on the final night, when Vice
President Agnew was nominated and he and the President, who
had been nominated the previous night, made their acceptance
speeches. The veterans, one of them in a wheel chair, displayed
end-the-war signs and tried a little heckling. Outside the hall, police doused hundreds of antiwar demonstrators with tear gas and,
there and elsewhere in Miami Beach, arrested hundreds. Remarkably, in view of their past readiness to make capital of disturbances
going on near them, neither Nixon nor Agnew took a crack at the
protesters. One got a notion, watching the Vice President and listening to his unmemorable speech, that he wouldn't mind being on
that or a similar podium in 1976, accepting the party's nomination
for the presidency.

The President's speech, hardly the historic document that the
convention chairman called it, provided a guide to what was coming in the campaign. George McGovern was going to catch it. The
President was going after him on the positions he took during the
primaries, not on the revised positions that he was preparing. On
Vietnam, while negotiations to end the war were proceeding,
Nixon would be taking the hard line so long as there was no
settlement. The country would be hearing often, beginning with
three campaign stops the day after he accepted the nomination,
about his journeys to Moscow and Peking and hopes of bringing
peace to the world if he were given another four years to do it.
Lines that he used in 1968 would be used in 1972: moving people
from welfare rolls to payrolls; supporting the peace forces against

the criminal forces; continual assurances that this is a great country and God's side was the side he was on and wanted the country
to stay on, with him. And there he was, the speech finished, standing with Agnew and singing "God Bless America."

A thought that I had in 1968, in this hall, came back. It was
that Agnew looks more like a President than Nixon does.

September 2, 1972

———

Weariness and deadline pressures caused me to underestimate
the Nixon and Agnew acceptance speeches. The Vice President's
memorable definition of his relationship to the President is quoted
in a later report. Mr. Nixon's clear projection of the positions he
took in the campaign and will be taking in his second term deserved notice it didn't get in the foregoing piece.

XXVI

Mesmerizing
the Press

San Clemente, California
The President was three minutes late for the "political press conference" that he promised last July to hold at the Western White House after he was nominated for a second term. His point when he described the promised session in that way was that he wouldn't abuse the presidency by exploiting the media for political purposes and answering questions about political matters until he was nominated and campaigning. It was an absurd point, not really intended to deceive anyone or to conceal the unconcealable fact that Richard Nixon has been campaigning for a second term since he was inaugurated in 1969. But after the spate of open campaigning that he began at a youth rally in Miami Beach the night he was nominated and continued with his intensely political acceptance speech and four appearances in Chicago, a Detroit suburb, San Diego and San Clemente the next day, I was interested in seeing how he would handle himself and how the press would handle him now that, for the first time in his 26 years in politics, he was both the President and a declared candidate.

He seemed to me to look a little tired but nonetheless chipper and sure of himself when, in a blue-gray suit that we hadn't seen before, he walked through the rows of magnificent flowers and bushes that adorn the lawn and gardens of his home beside the ocean to the spot, under towering palm and eucalyptus trees, where the reporters awaited him. There, after a few moments of silence while news photographers had at him—no film or sound recording for broadcast was permitted—he proceeded to put on and get by with a display of mixed gall and skill that I've never seen equaled.

The occasion for the display was the accumulated and ever-blackening news of skullduggery in the collection and use of Nixon campaign funds and in a closely related matter, the electronic bugging of the Democratic National Committee headquarters in Washington last summer. The main facts, familiar though they are, must be summarized if the Nixon performance is to be sufficiently appreciated.

Five men were caught June 17 in the act of installing or removing—probably removing—listening equipment from the ceiling of an office adjoining that of then Democratic National Chairman Lawrence O'Brien. One of them was the chief security officer of the Committee for the Reelection of the President (renamed the other day the Committee to Reelect President Nixon). This committee was directed at the time by former Attorney General John Mitchell and is directed now by Clark MacGregor, who moved from the White House staff to the campaign job when Mitchell resigned. Most of MacGregor's key assistants are recruits from the White House staff. He and those assistants look to H. R. Haldeman, the President's staff chief, for daily guidance and direction. Campaign funds and former Commerce Secretary Maurice Stans, the President's chief money-raiser in this and the 1968 campaign, have been in the bugging picture since July. A total of $114,000 in campaign contributions got from Stans through devious and as yet undisclosed channels, some of them threading through Mexico, to Bernard Barker, a shadowy Miami businessman with CIA connections who was one of the five men caught in June. Part of the $114,000, a check for $25,000, turns out to have been contributed originally in cash by Dwayne Andreas, a Minneapolis businessman who has been previously known as the chief financial supporter of Senator Hubert Humphrey.

One of the several agencies looking into this welter of campaign oddities is the General Accounting Office, an independent investigative arm of Congress. It monitors compliance with a new federal election law which requires among other things that donations of

" HE SAYS HE'S FROM THE PHONE COMPANY ... "

$100 and more to national campaigns after last April 7 be reported to GAO, with the donors identified. The givers of some $10 million to the Nixon campaign were promised anonymity if they ponied up before April 7, and both Stans and the President have made it evident that they consider themselves bound by that promise. Two days after Mr. Nixon was nominated, the GAO reported to the Justice Department that an audit of Nixon committee funds had uncovered nine instances of possible or "apparent" violations of the new election law, most of them involving incomplete or nonexistent records and confusion as to whether large sums, including the $25,000 from Andreas, were actually contributed after the April 7 deadline. The GAO reported to the Justice Department that it could find no records showing the source of $350,000 that was kept in cash in a safe in Stans' committee office as late as May 25. For political sophisticates, this was the most damning note in the GAO findings. There is a stench over campaign cash in such amounts, inviting questions as to where it comes from and what it's for and why banks and traceable checks are avoided by donors and collectors.

Such, in barest outline, was the situation that the President-candidate knew he was going to be asked about when he stood under his palm trees on a sunny morning in San Clemente. Some of the reporters thought that he tensed up and seemed nervous as he dealt with the few questions thrown at him about it. He seemed to me to be totally cool, totally in command of himself and his questioners. He began: "With regard to the handling of campaign funds, we have a new law here in which technical violations have occurred and are occurring, apparently, on both sides." That was the tone of all the replies. Maurice Stans, "an honest man and one who is very meticulous," was investigating the matter "very, very thoroughly, because he doesn't want any evidence at all to be outstanding, indicating that we have not complied with the law." As for the bugging, the FBI and the Justice Department and his own staff counsel, John Dean, were investigating it and he, the President, could say categorically "that no one in the White House staff, no one in this administration presently employed, was involved in this very bizarre incident."

The reporters never caught him up on his saving phrase, "presently employed." John Mitchell and a lesser figure, Hugh Sloan, who formerly worked for Bob Haldeman at the White House and had been fingered by Maurice Stans as the committee assistant to whom the $25,000 check was passed, had quit the committee. Mitchell had fired another assistant, also a former White House employee, who had refused to answer FBI questions. The President was not asked whether he had any or all of them or somebody else in mind. He was not asked, either, whether with all of these investigations going on he now knew who had ordered the bugging and why it was ordered. I stood within 10 feet of him and didn't even try to ask that simple and obvious question. The press conference was almost over when a reporter recalled to the President his smooth and passing reference to "technical violations" of the campaign funds law "on both sides" and said, "I was just wondering what Democratic violations you had in mind." Mr. Nixon was as bland and calm as ever when he replied: "I think that will come out in the balance of this week. I will let the political people talk about that, but I understand that there have been [violations] on both sides."

Other questions were asked and answered. The President appeared to be utterly tough and unyielding on the Vietnam war, among other things implicitly correcting Defense Secretary Melvin Laird's statement the previous day that the bombing of North Vietnam and the mining of its harbors would be ended if the North Vietnamese withdrew their forces from South Vietnam and stopped transporting equipment and reinforcements across the north-south border at the Demilitarized Zone. "Absolutely not," the President said when he was asked if anything short of negotiated settlement on his latest terms would bring an end of the bombing and mining. He was going to campaign hard as if the polls didn't show him so far ahead of George McGovern that he might be forgiven for treating the election as a mere formality. He would do it mostly from the White House, being President, and apart from occasional one-day political forays would not really hit the stump until the last three weeks before November 7. But the thing I'll always remember about Mr. Nixon's first "political press conference" of 1972 was his handling of the funds and bugging matter and our failure to handle him as a vulnerable candidate should have been handled. It was a lesson in the mesmerizing power of the presidency.

September 9, 1972

XXVII

Mandate Wanted

Near the close of the President's August 29 press conference in California, he spoke with some incoherence and great earnestness of a feeling that he has about the country and of why he hopes to be reelected by the popular majority that the voters denied him in 1968. The feeling that he expressed, not very clearly, is that the country has recovered from the assassinations and other turmoils that were tearing it apart four years ago and is ready now for "a new sense of mission, a new sense of confidence, a new sense of purpose as to where we are going." Although his actual words were that a new sense of mission, confidence and purpose is "what we need in this country," he seemed to me to be trying to say that the country not merely needs such a new sense but is ready for it and he is the leader who can supply it. After a defensive digression into what he and his administration are and are not ("the President of the United States is not the number-one war-maker of the world"), he said that he was coming "back to the point" and did so in these words: "We need a mandate, therefore, in which the President receives a clear majority. We are going to work for a clear majority and as big a one as we can get. We don't assume that it is going to be big, but it will be clear because there is not a third party candidate of significance."

Here was a guide to the kind of campaign that Mr. Nixon intends to conduct and is requiring his managers and surrogates to arrange. The objective is the biggest attainable majority for the President. A Nixon majority comes ahead, way ahead, of *Republican* majorities for Senate, House, gubernatorial and other party candidates. A perception that this is true was one of the few divisive and troubling factors at the Miami Beach convention. The fights over future convention rules and procedure were enlivened and at times embittered by the obvious apprehension of many delegates that the welfare of the Republican Party was being subordinated to the welfare and anticipated triumph of Richard Nixon. Campaign funds are being collected and allotted primarily for a Nixon victory. The instrument relied upon to accomplish the victory is not the Republican National Committee but the White House adjunct that can't decide whether to call itself the Committee for the Reelection of the President, the Committee to Reelect the President, or the Committee to Reelect President Nixon. The day after he was renominated, Nixon urged young first-time voters in Utica, Michigan, to "get into the game" regardless of whether they are for him. His reelection committee, organizing a massive drive to register potential voters, takes a different tack. The committee's deputy director, Fred Malek, said last week that the million volunteer canvassers it hopes to mobilize are being told to "pass on to the next house" if they encounter citizens who aren't for Nixon.

When Senator Hugh Scott of Pennsylvania, the Republican minority leader, was asked at the White House the other day what the President plans to do by way of campaigning "on behalf of Republican candidates in the Senate," the most he could say was that he expects Mr. Nixon to make "a suitable announcement" in due course. The President indicated at his California press conference that he'd like to have a new Congress with Republican majorities in both houses but understands that the more realistic hope is for "a new majority in Congress made up of Republicans and Democrats who support what the President believes in." He also indicated something less than total confidence that a Republican Congress would be more likely than a Democratic Congress to enact Nixon legislation. The chief advantage to him, he suggested, would be that "at least we could have responsibility for leadership." Given the practical certainty that Republican majorities in the Senate and House would include a sizable proportion of conservatives who regard Mr. Nixon as a crypto-liberal and distrust much of his foreign and domestic policy, I suspect that the President prefers a Congress dominated by Democrats who may discern in a decisive majority of popular votes for him the "positive mandate" that he longs for and may be moved by it to "support what the President believes in." He came close to admitting as much when he remarked in California, "I am honest enough to say that there are several Democrats in the House and several (Democratic) senators without whose support I could not have conducted the foreign policy of the United States over these past four years."

The emphasis upon a maximum popular majority for the President explains a good deal of otherwise odd behavior around and near Mr. Nixon. At a time when the polls predict a Nixon landslide and might be expected to instill overwhelming confidence in his spokesmen, they have been acting as if they were a pack of frightened losers. What alarms them is not the prospect of defeat —few if any of them believe that is possible—but another narrow victory comparable to the one in 1968, when 43.4 percent of the popular vote gave Nixon 301 of 538 electoral college votes. The President is telling his people to ignore the enormous spread of 30 points and more indicated for him over McGovern in the national polls and to heed instead the margins, running around eight to 10 points, indicated in such big and critical states as California, Illinois, Pennsylvania and New York. That's good for now, he is saying, but it's too close for complacence when the hazards of this or any campaign are considered. He's saying that he will be unhappy with less than 55 percent of the popular vote on November 7 and delighted with anything over that. The gist of his private admonitions is that the result is almost certain to be considerably closer than the national polls predict and that the "positive mandate" he seeks has to be fought for as fiercely as it would have to be if he were the probable loser.

This is why the Nixon pose of a cool and confident incumbent, giving first priority at this stage of the campaign to his "responsibilities to conduct the presidency," cracked open during the three weeks after he was renominated. Senator George McGovern's charge that big grain traders had advance and inside knowledge of the Soviet Union's huge and unexpected purchases of American wheat and did farmers out of millions in profits from rising prices could have been ridden out in stolid silence, on the reasonably safe assumption that most voters would conclude that it's the sort of thing that naturally happens in an enterprise economy. Instead, Secretary of Agriculture Earl Butz bellowed denial after denial, thus furthering the impression that Senator McGovern had touched a sore nerve and that the administration had something to hide. The intense White House and reelection committee reaction to the Democrats' skillful play upon the electronic bugging of their national committee offices and the Republican reluctance to identify the contributors of $10 million or more in Nixon campaign money similarly served to magnify rather than diminish the impression that people who are very close indeed to Richard Nixon are responsible for serious political malfeasance.

Perhaps the most revealing show of excessive anxiety, however, was the staged and, on its face, ridiculous pledge that a second Nixon administration will not recommend increases in anybody's federal taxes if the President is reelected. On a single day at the White House, Congressman Gerald Ford of Michigan and Press Secretary Ronald Ziegler and John D. Ehrlichman, the assistant for domestic affairs, were trotted forth in succession to assert and justify this insupportable pledge. The performance was intended to promote the campaign theme that "a vote for George McGovern is a vote for higher taxes." That is probably true, but the President's spokesmen talked themselves into an awful and unnecessary tangle with their transparent effort to make the most of what they take to be a popular line and a useful point against McGovern. Ehrlichman, the principal promoter of the line, had to acknowledge that circumstances beyond the President's control may require an increase in federal taxes and that Mr. Nixon's rather vague undertaking to enable states and localities to reduce property taxes cannot be fulfilled unless additional sources of federal revenue are found. Ehrlichman tried to but couldn't talk his way around the plain fact that the new tax reforms that the President keeps promising and failing to disclose after 19 months of study are bound to entail increases in some federal taxes and decreases in others if they are to be meaningful. All in all, the performance amounted to a sorry display of avoidable confusion and provided evidence in proof of the cliché that if anybody can blow the prospective Nixon victory, it's Richard Nixon.

September 23, 1972

XXVIII

Agnew's Dilemma

Every now and then, during a week of travel with Spiro T. Agnew in his first open campaigning for the Republican ticket, I dug out the text of his speech accepting his renomination at Miami Beach and read this passage at the beginning of it: "I have lived in the crucible that is the Vice Presidency for nearly four years. And I have come to believe that, notwithstanding its simple constitutional definition, the office has two primarily important functions —to serve the President and to learn from the President. Surely, much of the controversy about the Vice Presidency could be quieted if we would accept the fact that the Vice President is the President's man and not a competing political entity. He accepts the investiture of Presidential trust, runs on the same platform, and must be a man upon whom the President can depend for total loyalty and support. He is a part of the President's team, contributing candidly his best advice in the formulation of policies and, once these policies are formulated, helping translate them into achievements. That is the way I view the office and I believe that is the true meaning of the 12th Amendment, which for 184 years has required that the President and Vice President run together and be elected as a team."

The thought came, watching Agnew and listening to him at

rallies and press conferences in Minnesota, Missouri, Ohio, Tennessee, North Carolina, Virginia and Kentucky, that being "the President's man" is not and never has been as easy for him as he tries to make it appear to be. The difficulty is not a matter of loyalty to Richard Nixon, or even of affection for him. Mr. Agnew probably would acknowledge that he was indulging in campaign hyperbole when he told a partisan crowd in Chattanooga, "I'm here to speak for the reelection of the greatest President this country has ever had—Richard Nixon." But he sounded to me like a man who was expressing the truth as he knew it when he continued, "And I want to assure you that my speaking for President Nixon is a labor of love, because there is no question that he has understood the role of a Vice President better than any President in the history of this country."

The Vice President's difficulty is that he is trying to be two men at once, his own man and the President's man. Pride aside, and pride in himself is one of Spiro Agnew's obvious characteristics, it is more essential to him now than it has previously been that he appear to the country to be his own man. It is essential to him because he hopes and intends to be nominated for the presidency and elected President in 1976. He denies that this is true when it is so simply and directly stated, but a week on the campaign road with him convinced me that it is true. In the course of campaigning for the President's reelection and, more emphatically and explicitly than Richard Nixon has shown any sign of doing, for Republican congressional and state candidates, Spiro Agnew seeks to portray himself to the country as a Vice President who is fit to be the President that he could become by succession at any moment and wants to become by election in 1976. His denials that he has decided to go for the presidency next time are qualified by the admission that he intends to "keep the option" and that he wouldn't be standing for reelection to the vice presidency this year if he didn't "consider the possibility of seeking the presidency in 1976."

At Minneapolis, the first stop on his 1972 campaign tour, Mr. Agnew was asked whether his announced and visible change of style, from extreme and savage and often divisive denunciation to a studied attempt at moderation, is "connected in any way with the desire to be (elected) President in 1976" and he answered "No." I didn't believe it and I doubt that any of the reporters who

" ISN'T THE THE ONE WHO SAID M°GOVERN WAS WRONG
TO GO BEGGING ON HIS KNEES TO THE ENEMY ? "

heard him believed it. What I do believe, and urge one and all to believe, is that the Vice President speaks the whole truth when he says that he is the same old Spiro Agnew. Here is how he said it in Minneapolis: "I have not changed any principle, any major principle on which I campaigned for governor (of Maryland), on which I campaigned for Vice President in 1968, or on which I campaigned for others in 1970. I make no apology for anything I said in any of those campaigns. I regret that some of the things were misunderstood, perhaps. And I regret that connotations were placed around some of the more colorful rhetoric I may have used that I thought were not really indicated by my standards. However, I respect the right of other people to apply their standards to what I say. I'm trying this year to adopt a new style, a style that will not bring about these misconstructions of my intent. I'm also trying to place the emphasis in the campaign on very well established and logical and substantiated positions that I can substantiate because I have to live with them, and believe in them, and my record is there to prove it. So, it's a question of emphasis and style. It's not a question of changing my principles."

Looking at and listening to Mr. Agnew when he said this, I had no doubt whatever that he meant every word of it and really believed that he not only could but was entitled to dismiss in that fashion, to relegate to limbo, his previous attacks on "radiclibs," "impudent snobs," "rotten apples," biased and dishonorable media elitists, the entire lexicon of invective with which he had polarized the nation and aroused the hatred and contempt which he now seeks to dispel. I had no doubt, either, that he was getting by with it and probably would continue to get by with it. A fact that has to be reported is that he did it very well, quietly and pleasantly and, for any who could forget his recent past as easily as he proposed to dismiss it, in a rather appealing way. In order to understand how this can be said, you have to picture him at his press conferences, seated in a low chair, immaculately groomed and tailored, right leg crossed over left leg, right hand at rest on right thigh, his tanned and nobly proportioned head held high, smiling his thin smile and talking in his habitual monotone. He was downright likeable when he was asked how he felt about the new style and answered: "Well, I like it. I like the way it is being received and it is very comfortable for me. It has many advantages and lets me get to the issues, and it obviates answering all the

questions about my rhetoric, which never did appeal to me." A
reporter interjected, "The rhetoric or the questions, Mr. Vice President?" and he answered, "Neither." The truth is that he relished
the rhetoric and loathed the questions.

The trouble with the revised Agnew is that he remains Agnew.
In my opinion, which he seemed to me to justify during the week
on the road, this is to say that he remains a man of considerable
presence and limited intelligence. Two examples from the first of
four press conferences in five days will suffice. He had barely
completed his profession of dedication to "the issues" and to
"substantiated positions" when, in the midst of a long disclaimer
that anybody in a responsible job at the White House or at the
affiliated Nixon reelection committee had anything to do with the
famous bugging of the Democrats' national headquarters in Washington last summer, he said: "I have a personal theory that I can't
substantiate, and that is that somebody set up these people that
were involved in this strictly for political use. . . . What I'm saying
is that someone set up these people and encouraged them to
undertake this caper, encouraged them to embarrass the Republican Party." In a reference to the former Democratic national
chairman and present McGovern campaign director, Lawrence
O'Brien, who has maintained that people very near to Richard
Nixon had to be responsible for the bugging, the Vice President
also said, "Now, I'm engaging in the same sort of wild fancy that
Mr. O'Brien is engaging in. I predicated my remarks by explaining
to you that I had no information or facts, but that I didn't think he
had, either." Then and in subsequent press conferences, when
questioners plagued him with demands that he substantiate his
"wild fancy," the Vice President never once indicated the slightest
awareness that he had made a fool of himself with a silly display
of inconsistency. The sub rosa explanation, offered by his staff,
that his "personal theory" had actually originated at the White
House and that the campaign tacticians ensconced there had encouraged him to throw out the notion of a Democratic plant,
proved upon inquiry to do him no more credit than the public
performance had. There is a suspicion at the White House, perhaps imparted to Mr. Agnew, that the alleged discovery of a faulty
telephone bug, announced by the Democrats weeks after the major

act of espionage had been uncovered, was a heinous device to magnify the embarrassment of the Republicans. If he did expound his wild fancy at White House suggestion, which is quite likely, the Vice President blew the limited suspicion just described into a farcical implication that Democrats rather than Republicans were responsible for the entire affair.

The other example is Mr. Agnew's flat statement that the President had ordered the FBI to investigate the possibility that grain dealers with inside and improper information profited inordinately from the recent wheat sales to Russia. That investigation, he said, "is in progress." It was not in progress when he said it was; it is extremely doubtful that it had been ordered or seriously contemplated when he said it had been instituted; and the mishmash of White House and Agnew staff explanations that followed his statement suggests very strongly that the President finally authorized the investigation in order to cover up an Agnew fumble. The last thing the Nixon administration needed at that point was another investigation of itself by itself. Three other executive and congressional investigations of the Soviet grain deal were already in progress. A Vice President who is as smart as Mr. Agnew naturally wants himself thought to be would have been on the radiophone from his chartered Boeing plane, urging his White House mentors not to be stupid instead of—as his spokesmen claimed—getting authoritative word that a superfluous investigation had been ordered and started.

Apart from any indications of intelligence or lack of the same that these episodes may provide, they bear upon the Vice President's desire and endeavor to appear to be his own man on his own in the 1972 campaign. With some pronounced misgivings at upper White House staff levels, the Vice President has been allowed to play his campaign role without the direct White House supervision that he had to put up with in 1970. The Agnew staff takes outspoken pride in the fact that not a single Nixon assistant or adviser is with the Vice President on his campaign travels. It is well understood at the White House that only the President may order the Vice President to say or do anything. It is equally well understood that White House staff suggestions will be received and treated with respect when they are conveyed to the Vice President. The tone and content of his attacks on George McGovern, for instance, accurately reflect White House guidance and

tell more about Richard Nixon than they do about Spiro Agnew.
A minor question raised by the less impressive aspects of the first
Agnew week on the road is whether guidance by remote suggestion is sufficient. The major question is whether Mr. Agnew is
fitted to be either Vice President or President. My doubts on that
score survived the week with him.

October 7, 1972

———

At the turn of 1972/73, the Vice President relinquished his responsibilities for federal-state cooperation and communication to
the White House staff, and his personal staff was sharply reduced.
So was the total Nixon staff, but not the President's immediate and
personal staff.

XXIX

Up the Wall

Readers say in letters that they are variously shocked, angered, horrified, insulted, devastated, dismayed and appalled by my confession in *The New Republic's* September 9 issue that I stood within 10 feet of Mr. Nixon at a press conference in California and didn't even try to ask him a simple and obvious question about the bugging of the Democratic Party's Washington headquarters. The complainants raise a subject that other people including Senator McGovern, President Nixon and David Broder, a political reporter and columnist for *The Washington Post*, have also raised. The subject is the nature of the responsibility of reporters who specialize in the coverage of Richard Nixon now that he is both an incumbent President and a candidate for reelection. Senator McGovern says that reporters should be telling the country that the President hides from public debate, lies to handpicked crowds, and refuses to hold press conferences and answer questions that should be put to him and answered. Mr. Nixon says in effect that reporters should recognize the justice of his claim that at this stage of the 1972 campaign his first responsibility is to do his job as President of the United States and accept without cavil his statement that "I shall campaign only when I conclude it will not interfere with doing the job the people elected me to do." David Broder, one of the best political reporters in the business, writes that "the Nixon entourage seems to be stifling the kind of dialogue that has in the past been thought to be the heart of a presidential campaign" and argues that "the press of the country ought to be calling Mr. Nixon on this—not for George McGovern's sake but for the sake of its own tattered reputation and for the public which it presumes to serve."

Herewith, in the faint hope that I won't seem to be unbearably defensive and pompous, I set forth my conception of the reporter's responsibility as it applies to me and describe my way of trying to meet it. My text is a portion of a letter from a reader in Freeport, NY. The reader didn't answer his telephone when he was called several times to ask permission to use his name and he therefore is quoted without further identification. He writes: "I am in no position to look into President Nixon's eyes and ask him to explain the contradictory statements and conduct that flow from his administration of our government. But you are. I am in no position to question Vice President Agnew when he censures the patriotism of those who disagree with Mr. Nixon's handling of the Vietnam war. But you are. These men, and their peers, should be pushed up any available wall to defend openly and honestly their policies, foreign and domestic. They should be asked and asked and asked by reporters such as yourself until some measure of truth begins to creep out. I am anxious to know why so many good reporters, who face President Nixon and his workers every day, are intimidated by the man and what he stands for. Is he so awesome that he is beyond question? Why were you, Mr. Osborne, afraid to ask that simple and obvious question of Mr. Nixon?"

Well, hell's fire, I wasn't afraid to ask the question. Respect for the presidency and a sense of the futility of trying to make this President say anything he doesn't want to say do have the mesmerizing effect noted in my California report. But that is not intimidation. Asking public questions at public press conferences just isn't my way of reporting. I occasionally throw a question at the President's press secretary, Ronald Ziegler, at his regular White House briefings, and it may be said with confidence that Ziegler rarely enjoys the questions. I recall three occasions when I tried to catch the President's eye and be recognized for a question at some of the 28 press conferences he has held to date. Recogni-

"WHEN THIS ELECTION'S OVER, DICK NIXON WON'T HAVE
THE PRESS TO KICK HIM AROUND ANYMORE!"

tion isn't easy to get in that mob of reporters; I didn't try very hard; and I doubt that the President even knew I was trying. I didn't try very hard for two reasons. They are that I prefer to do my serious questioning in private, with the various Nixon assistants who grant me audience now and then, and that I hold public press conferences in very low esteem.

The reader whom I have quoted is the victim of a common illusion, which is cultivated by the press in general and by most of my colleagues. The illusion is that press conferences, especially when they are conducted by so skillful an operator as Mr. Nixon, are really useful instruments of public information. They seldom are. Mr. Nixon has said several times that he regards the press conference as merely one means of communication with the public and that he has a right to choose it or any of his other means— statements, speeches, etc.—for communication. I concede him that right and exercise my right to draw certain conclusions from the fact that he has chosen to hold fewer press conferences than any of his recent predecessors. One of my conclusions, which will be considered heresy by most other reporters, is that the President does himself a disservice and does the country a service in holding so few press conferences. He would be worse off and the country would be better off if he didn't hold any press conferences. My reason for thinking this, already indicated, is that Mr. Nixon is altogether too good for the common good at using press conferences to present himself and his policies in a favorable light. He has been embarrassed at times by the sort of hard questions that he pretends to like and actually detests. He may have been driven to a few admissions of error that he didn't want to make. But I don't recall, and I don't find in a review of his conference transcripts, a single instance of a useful revelation that wasn't already available or didn't soon become available in other parts of the Nixon record. A demonstrable fact is that the hard questions do the President more good than harm when they are asked at televised press conferences. Broadcast reporters, who get much more mail than writing reporters do, are deluged with letters hostile to them and friendly to Mr. Nixon when they question him in a fashion that seems to many viewers to be disrespectful of the presidency. The President's success in using press conferences for his own ends is one of the reasons, I am convinced, for his lead over Senator McGovern in the national polls. This thought is commended to the senator, with the suggestion that he abandon his call upon Mr. Nixon to hold more press conferences. A suddenly called session in the President's office on October 5, his second press conference since he was renominated, did him no harm and McGovern no good.

I should confess at this point that my purpose in life is not to drive Mr. Nixon up the wall that my complaining readers want to see him pasted to. My purpose is to convey as clear a portrayal of him and his policies as I am capable of conveying. If the portrayal drives him up the wall, which I doubt, so be it. For me, there are two ways of accomplishing the purpose. Neither of them is pitching tough questions at the President in public. One way, the President being unavailable to the likes of me for private questioning, is to work hard at extracting whatever information and impressions I can from his phenomenally loyal and cautious assistants and from other officials. The other way is to search Mr. Nixon's considered statements, the kind he makes without reportorial prodding, for the substance of his policies and the volunteered reflection of his attitudes that they provide. I find in them very few of the lies that Senator McGovern accuses him of telling. I do find in them many inconsistencies, evasions and exaggerations, some cause for sustained distrust, and a good deal that has to be admired. One of the qualities to be found and documented in them is the President's talent for bland deception of his audiences. In Los Angeles on September 27, at a fund-raiser that produced the record sum of $1,755,000 for his campaign, the President said: "I was proud to be able to say, in addressing 124 nations at the International Monetary Fund meeting (in Washington) on Monday of this week, that the United States of America, at this time, had the lowest rate of inflation, the highest rate of growth, the highest real income of any industrial nation in the world." Mr. Nixon said nothing of the kind at the IMF meeting, where he knew his hearers knew the facts. What he said on that occasion was, "We are now experiencing one of the lowest rates of inflation, one of the highest rates of real economic growth, of any industrial nation." Compare the statements and think about them. That's what I try to do.

October 14, 1972

Cutting Up McGovern

A Nixon assistant, Patrick Buchanan, has on his desk a copy of Robert Sam Anson's biography of Senator George McGovern (*McGovern*—Holt, Rinehart & Winston; $7.95). Many passages are underlined. The one most heavily marked, the one Buchanan calls "that baby" and reads aloud with loving joy, quotes McGovern as follows on his unsuccessful effort to defeat Senator Karl Mundt of South Dakota in 1960: "It was my worst campaign. I hated him so much I lost my sense of balance. I was too negative. I made some careless charges. When the media in the state turned against me, the television and radio stations and almost all the newspapers, I got kind of rattled. I got on the defensive. I started explaining and answering things I should have ignored. It was hard to get a hook in Mundt."

McGovern on McGovern in this passage is one of the texts that Buchanan and the five other members of Richard Nixon's White House "attack group" rely upon in their daily, incessant watch upon the senator's campaign performance and their attendant effort to spot and make the most of his mistakes and weaknesses. In their roles as the working tacticians of the Nixon campaign, the assistants who provide Vice President Agnew, Cabinet members and some 50 lesser surrogates with ideas and suggestions for jabs

at McGovern, the members of the attack group are under orders
from the President and his staff chief, H. R. Haldeman, to keep
their assignment and even the office where they convene hidden
from the press. The senior attacker is Charles Colson, special
counsel to the President, a lawyer who spends a lot of time with
Mr. Nixon and none at all, nowadays, with reporters who have
him rightly tagged as the assistant in charge of dirty tricks. The
others are Ken W. Clawson, until last February a first-rate newspaper reporter who was recruited by Colson to be the President's
deputy director of communications; Pat Buchanan, a conservative
writer who is among the few genuine ideologues left among the
pragmatists in Nixon's service; Wallace Johnson, a White House
lobbyist who represents William Timmons, the chief lobbyist, in
the attack group; and Edward Failor, a special assistant to Clark
MacGregor, a former Minnesota congressman and White House
assistant who replaced former Attorney General John N. Mitchell
as the director of the Committee to Reelect the President after the
bugging of the Democratic headquarters was discovered last summer. Failor chairs the attack group in Colson's absence and is
regarded at the reelection committee, where the strong White
House hand is resented, as the group's dominant member. Albert
E. Abrahams, a public relations specialist who moved from the
staff of the President's Cost of Living Council to the committee
soon after MacGregor did, also sits with the group and acts for
MacGregor when Failor is occupied elsewhere.

The original assignment of the attack group was to get George
McGovern down. Now it is to keep him down. Its visible way of
doing this is to track his every word and action, partly from press
reports and partly from the personal and more or less covert
observation that occurs in all national political campaigns and has
been brought to an unprecedented level of skill and thoroughness
in the Nixon campaign. Nixon observers are present at every Mcgovern appearance just as—or so the Nixonites assume—
McGovern observers are at every Nixon and Nixon surrogate performance. The Nixon tacticians have arranged, as they assume
their McGovern counterparts have, to have friendly watchers and
informants in newspaper offices, television and radio studios and,
where and as they can manage it, among the opponent's workers
and supporters at campaign centers from the national headquarters down to precincts.

"LAST YEAR, HE SAID... THIS YEAR, HE SAID... LAST YEAR, HE SAID..."

This is standard campaign procedure, within accepted political norms. There is, however, factual basis for the impression that the Nixon people, endowed with more campaign money than is good for them and imbued with a driving ambition to amass for the President the biggest popular majority in recent times, have stretched the accepted procedures to extreme and, even by the loose standards of applied politics, dishonorable lengths. *The Washington Post* reported last week that FBI investigators of the Democratic headquarters bugging had come upon evidence of a deliberate and elaborate Republican effort to disrupt the Democratic primary campaigns and eliminate George McGovern's competitors for the nomination with hired spies and saboteurs. One of the *Post* allegations was that Ken Clawson, one of the attack group, had faked and personally written a published newspaper letter that contributed to the collapse of Senator Edmund Muskie's try for the nomination. Clawson came to the White House from the *Post*. One of his friends and former colleagues there, Marilyn Berger, said that he told her on September 25, "I wrote the letter." Clawson told his former editors, who didn't seem to believe him, that he had nothing to do with the letter and that Miss Berger must have misunderstood him. Miss Berger said that she didn't misunderstand him: "He said it and I stand by it." Beyond saying after prolonged questioning that Clawson still had the President's confidence, Press Secretary Ronald Ziegler refused to back up Clawson's denial with a White House denial. Ziegler's evident purpose, as it has been throughout the spate of reports and allegations about misused and secret campaign funds, electronic bugging and the like, is to keep the President as far as possible from the accumulating dirt pile. Clawson didn't offer to quit and wasn't asked to quit. He continued to go about his business in the attack operation with his usual aggressive skill.

The Colson-Clawson operation is remarkable in its visible aspects only for its deadly and thorough persistence. Its principal aim was and is to rob George McGovern of the asset that he has done so much to impair. The asset is (or was) his reputation for courage, decency and credibility. In the guidelines that go out from the attack group to Cabinet members, the Vice President and other high-ranking surrogate speakers for Nixon, and through the reelection committee to lesser spokesmen, the real or manufactured differences between the positions that McGovern took in his

primary campaigns and the modified positions that he takes now
are ruthlessly emphasized. The object is to depict him as an incon-
sistent and unstable radical, a waffler, a shrill weakling who by
nature and character is compelled to make the kind of mistakes he
confessed to making in the 1960 Mundt campaign. The immediate
architect of these tactics is Colson. The chief implementer and
frequent deviser of them is Clawson. The immediate overseer is
Bob Haldeman. The supreme and ever-watchful overseer of the
entire operation is President Nixon.

The President's part in the operation is never discussed or willingly disclosed at the White House. Three of his directives to the
attack group and to the many others involved in the operation are
known, however. One of his earliest orders was that, given a
choice of tone and manner, the harsh and vengeful note that he
himself struck in the ·1970 midterm campaign should be avoided
in favor of a gentler, low-key approach. Another was that the
words "Democratic" and "Democrats" be avoided whenever possible, except in references to Democrats for Nixon. The partisan
term was to be shunned with particular care in references to the
administration's congressional opposition and to the rivals of Republican candidates for Congress. A third Nixon order, the best
example of his intervention in specific situations, was that nobody
connected with him or his candidacy for reelection was to say a
word about Senator McGovern's decisions first to retain and then
to dump his first vice presidential nominee, Senator Thomas
Eagleton. The President appears to have perceived at the time,
sooner than most of his counselors did, that the Eagleton affair
would prove to be the disaster for McGovern that it has turned
out to be, the seemingly ineradicable evidence in the public mind
that he is indeed the indecisive and unstable changeling that the
White House attackers industriously try to make him out to be.

The single permitted departure from this general approach has
to do with McGovern's Vietnam and defense positions. On these,
he is depicted on the President's orders as a beggar for peace,
an advocate of surrender, a wrecker of essential national security. Mr. Nixon lets others say it, implies it himself, but never says
it directly of McGovern. The most interesting facet of the 1972
campaign is the way in which the Nixon pose of impersonal detachment has worked for him and against Senator McGovern. It
has had, all too often, the effect upon the senator that McGovern

hoped and is still trying to have upon Nixon. It is McGovern, not Nixon, who has been driven to the harsh and shrill extremes that have been Nixon trademarks. The ultimate irony is that they are in character for Richard Nixon, out of character for George Mc-Govern.

October 21, 1972

————

Some of the conductors of the attack operation felt and said, after the election, that their work had much more to do with the result than the press generally gave them credit for. They are welcome to the credit they claim.

It must be added that I was not so sure in early 1973 as I was in October that the "harsh and shrill extremes" were "out of character for George McGovern."

XXXI

Guilty Men

This account of the reaction at the Nixon White House and at its adjunct, the Committee for the Reelection of the President, to reports and allegations of campaign sabotage and spying on the President's behalf is written in awareness that the sordid business probably isn't going to make enough difference to matter on November 7. The signs three weeks before the election are that the voters are inclined to give Mr. Nixon his popular majority and that most of them don't give a damn about the evidence that some extremely devious means were employed to attain it for him. The reaction reported here seems likely to amount in retrospect to nothing more than a footnote to the Nixon story, a minor testament to his talents as a reader of the public mind and conscience and to the efficacy of the protective apparatus and techniques which he and some of the men who serve him have been perfecting since he was inaugurated in 1969. But, in all its comic triviality and sinister implications, the account is worth setting down for what it tells about Mr. Nixon and about one aspect of his approach to the responsibilities and hazards of the presidency.

On October 16, the day of reaction that concerns us here, the situation that confronted the President and his spokesmen was as follows. A spate of newspaper and magazine reports and allegations asserted among other things that Dwight L. Chapin, the President's appointments secretary, had hired Donald Segretti, a California lawyer and college classmate, to spy upon and sabotage Democratic primary campaigns and that Herbert Kalmbach, a prominent California attorney and Republican activist who has handled some of Mr. Nixon's private affairs, had passed to Segretti more than $35,000 in money, $25,000 of it in one cash payment, that had come originally from the Nixon reelection committee. *The Washington Post, Time* and *The New York Times* attributed these and related reports to "federal investigators," "information in the Justice Department's files," and a Los Angeles friend of Segretti's named Lawrence Young. There was much more to the reports, amounting in sum to a showing that the electronic bugging of the Democratic national headquarters in Washington last summer was merely the first discovered indication of a massive Republican effort, dating back to mid-1971 and directed from the White House, to disrupt the campaigns of rivals for the Democratic nomination for the presidency and, once a nominee had been chosen, to confuse and weaken his election effort. So far, there had been no hard evidence that the President himself was involved in or even knew about the manifold skullduggeries. The newly reported involvement of Chapin and Kalmbach and particularly of Chapin, one of the President's closest personal assistants, brought the business to the very door of the Oval Office. Through the White House press staff, Chapin acknowledged only that he had "known Donald Segretti since college days" and said that *The Washington Post* story which first connected him with Segretti's campaign work was "based on hearsay" and was "fundamentally inaccurate." The statement was far short of a convincing denial; it was given orally and only to the *Post;* and after making it Chapin took cover. He said, "I don't propose to have any further comment," and he didn't. Further comment was left to the President's press secretary, Ronald Ziegler, at his regular White House briefing on the 16th. The following excerpts from the official transcript of his duel with the press are condensed but convey the flavor and context.

"*Q*: Did Dwight Chapin hire Segretti to do political sabotage?

" FOUR MORE WEEKS !... FOUR MORE WEEKS !... "

"*A*: Mr. Chapin has made a comment on that and I don't have anything to add to it.

"*Q*: Is the President concerned about the report?

"*A*: The President is concerned about the techniques being applied by the opposition in the stories themselves. I would say his concern goes to the fact that stories are being run that are based on hearsay, innuendo, guilt by association.

"*Q*: Who is the opposition?

"*A*: Well, I think the opposition is clear. You know, since the Watergate (Democratic bugging) case broke, people have been trying to link the case with the White House . . . and no link has been established . . . because no link exists. Since that time the opposition has been making charges which are not substantiated, stories have been written which are not substantiated, stories have been written that are based upon hearsay and on sources that will not reveal themselves and all of this is being intermingled into an allegation that this administration, as the opposition points out, is corrupt. . . . That is what I am referring to and I am not going to comment on that type of story.

"*Q*: Why won't you deny the charges?

"*A*: I am not going to dignify these types of stories with a comment. . . . It goes without saying that this administration does not condone sabotage or espionage or surveillance of individuals, but it also does not condone innuendo or source stories that make broad sweeping charges about the character of individuals.

"*Q*: Are you saying that reporters should not seek out and use information obtained from such sources as Justice Department officials willing to discuss Justice Department reports and should accept and use only information provided by official spokesmen such as yourself?

"*A*: Absolutely not. The press has a right, every right, to probe for information, but I have a right to my opinion of how that information is used.

"*Q*: Would Dwight Chapin still be working here for the President if the President had any reason whatsoever to believe that he had hired Segretti for the purposes reported in these stories?

"*A*: I will simply answer your question by saying the President has confidence in Mr. Chapin."

The second reaction that day came from Clark MacGregor, the reelection committee's director, at the committee offices just up and across Pennsylvania Avenue from the White House. His reaction was to denounce *The Washington Post* for "hypocrisy" and to suggest that its relentless probing of Republican campaign tactics was done in the service of "the political elitist movement known as McGovernism." MacGregor, a former congressman and Nixon assistant who values the esteem of Washington reporters and was clearly embarrassed by the day's assignment, refused to take questions and staged his performance for television cameras. It was a weird performance, transparently omitting any meaningful denial of the reports he professed to be answering and substituting for denial a crude attack upon the credibility of one of the reporting newspapers. Ziegler was asked the next day whether MacGregor was in touch with the President before the performance was staged. In a rare and astonishing lapse from the protective process that usually shields Richard Nixon, the press secretary answered, "I would think so." Still later, Ziegler said that nobody on the White House staff had "directed" campaign sabotage, spying and espionage. Was he thereby denying that Dwight Chapin had hired and received reports from a campaign saboteur and spy? Ziegler wouldn't say yes or no.

The President had nothing to say, during the days of reaction dealt with here, in direct response to the reports of what his guilty men had been up to. But he did say two things that bear upon the subject. He spoke of the duty of "opinion leaders . . . the great editors and publishers and commentators and the rest" to "understand the importance of great decisions and the necessity to stand by the President of the United States when he makes a terribly difficult, unpopular decision." He was talking about his decision last May to bomb and mine North Vietnam, and the press criticism he got for it. But the remark could fairly be read as a reflection of a feeling that the press really doesn't have any business associating a President, however indirectly, with such dirty stuff as campaign spying and sabotage. This President, after all, was the one who had just said in a paid campaign broadcast: "I will work unceasingly to halt the erosion of moral fiber in American life, and the denial of individual account-ability for individual actions." The shady fringe of his own campaign could be a good place to do that work.

October 28, 1972

I learned later that Clark MacGregor was not at all "embarrassed by the day's assignment." He welcomed it and continued the same tactics on White House orders. Ziegler announced December 18 that the President was "very pleased" to keep Dwight Chapin on the second-term staff. Soon afterward, Chapin quit and a Senate committee received FBI evidence that the reports involving him were true.

XXXII

Reluctant Campaigner

Two of the few people admitted to the Westchester County Airport at White Plains, New York, in the early afternoon of October 23 were Governor and Mrs. Nelson Rockefeller. They arrived by car at 1:25 p.m., five minutes before the President and Mrs. Nixon arrived from Washington in the President's jet. Reporters who had preceded the Nixons in a chartered press plane surrounded the governor and asked him what difference he thought the President's afternoon of campaigning would make in Westchester County. "Well," the governor said, grinning rather slyly, "he's never spent that much time in Westchester before this." It wasn't much of a dig or much of a joke. But the reporters and Rockefeller laughed together, enjoying for a moment the mild reminder that the President had spent very little time campaigning anywhere since he was renominated in August and that he and the governor had been rivals for the Republican nomination in 1960 and 1968. The moment passed and Governor Rockefeller scurried to the foot of the presidential ramp and looked up, all aglow in new alliance, at the Nixons as they emerged from their plane for the President's fourth day in two months of campaigning in the traditional sense.

One of the numerous assistants, Secret Service agents and other

functionaries who also debarked from the President's plane was
Dwight L. Chapin, the appointments secretary. Aged 30, handsome, superbly groomed, Dwight Chapin is always with the President on his travels. He behaved on this afternoon exactly as he
always does, dashing toward and hopping into a car marked "Pilot
1" and, in it, taking his place near the head of the Nixon motorcade. There was something special about his presence this time,
however. It was the President's way of showing that he didn't
believe, or didn't care if he perchance did know and believe, that
his man Chapin had taken part in recruiting political spies and
saboteurs to disrupt the Democrats' primary campaigns. Close by
the President, as always, was H.R. (Bob) Haldeman, the chief of
the White House staff and the chief, too, of Mr. Nixon's political
operatives. Bob Haldeman is Dwight Chapin's boss. Everyone in
and around the White House assumes it to be a fact that Chapin
would never do anything of the sort he had recently been accused
of doing and hadn't denied doing if he didn't have Haldeman's
authority to do it. Within 36 hours of the New York appearance,
Haldeman would be said in a published report to have been one of
the five Nixon associates who controlled the use of the campaign
funds that were alleged to finance the spying and sabotage and
would be saying through the White House press staff that the
report "is untrue." *The Washington Post* reported in somewhat
ambiguous terms that Hugh W. Sloan, Jr., a former assistant to
Haldeman, had sworn to a grand jury that Haldeman was involved
in financing the sabotage operation from Nixon campaign funds.
Press Secretary Ronald Ziegler, speaking for the President, said
that Sloan had denied through his attorney that his testimony
implicated Haldeman and others mentioned in the *Post* report.
Throughout the afternoon and evening of attendance in New
York, Haldeman seemed to be his usual stern and confident self,
filming Mr. Nixon's every move with a home movie camera and
adding to what by now must be the largest private film collection
in White House history.

It was, all in all, the ordinary beginning of a strange afternoon
and evening. The President, motorcading for more than three
hours through 12 Westchester towns and villages, appeared to be
preoccupied and tense behind the synthetic Nixon smile. The

crowds along the streets and at the downtown squares and inter-
sections were big and for the most part friendly, never overtly
hostile. He left his car five times, was appropriately mobbed, and
shook countless hands, once when he was standing in his open-top
limousine and moving at 20 miles an hour. It was Veterans Day
and he justifiably called the total throng "really a warm, friendly
holiday crowd." McGovern supporters were out in force with enlarged photo-portraits of their candidate, pictures of Vietnamese
dead in ugly heaps, and signs challenging their visitor to come
clean about the sabotage and campaign funds charges. But there
were many more Nixon signs, many of them held aloft by children
and young adults who seemed to be as ardent for their man as
McGovern supporters were for theirs.

Yet it seemed to some of the trailing reporters, this one included, that Mr. Nixon endured it all as if he were fulfilling a
burdensome and repellent duty. His mind and true care seemed to
be elsewhere. At a reception for some 200 Republican workers
from the northeastern states at the Rockefeller family's Pocantico
Hills estate, after the Westchester motorcade was over, he called
in a dreary drone for his hearers to "get out the vote" and back
Republican state and congressional tickets "up and down." He
referred as follows to his coming appearances that evening at
rallies in two Long Island counties: "I am going to be speaking a
little later over at Nassau—is this Nassau? I am going to speak at
Nassau and Suffolk, in Nassau. So we are now in Westchester."

The President's mind could have been, and most of us supposed
it was, on Vietnam and the spate of peace rumors that he and his
roving assistant, Henry Kissinger, had been stimulating since nomination time in August. Reporters on the President's plane were
told during the flight from Washington that Kissinger had ended
five days of secret talks with Thieu in Saigon and was on his way
home. They were told that night that the President would confer
with Kissinger as soon as the Nixon party returned to Washington,
and again the next day. Remarkably, considering that it was Veterans Day and that on this day as always the President put predominant emphasis upon his quest for world peace, he referred
only once in his three set speeches, and then only in a passing
fragment of a sentence, to "the progress we have made in ending
the war in Vietnam, with honor and not surrender." Mr. Nixon in
New York surely knew in essence what Kissinger had to tell him

about the latest round of talks with the North Vietnamese in Paris and with President Thieu in Saigon, and didn't deem it fit for campaign use.

There could have been, and I suspect there were, two reasons for the President's unease and preoccupation. They were, in my guess, the state of the Vietnam negotiations and the cumulative campaign scandal. At a monster rally that evening, in a huge auditorium hard by the Nassau County airport, the war issue and the scandal issue hit Richard Nixon as nothing had hit him for months and he didn't like it. Three tiny bands of hecklers among 16,000 people in the hall messed up what should have been a triumphant occasion for him. Two of the groups were antiwar, one was pro-McGovern. Six or so antiwar shouters got into a fight with Nixon supporters and were thrown out by the police. Ten others, billing themselves Vietnam veterans, chanted "Peace now" and "Stop the bombing" and one of them yelled "Killer!" at measured intervals. They stood within 100 feet of the President, at his front and right, and they shook him as I haven't seen him shaken since the 1970 midterm campaign. He glared at them but never mentioned them and he had to pause, time and time again, when the crowd around the hecklers tried to drown their cries with counter-chants of "Four more years!" Perhaps 20 pro-McGovern youngsters, just behind the antiwar veterans, contented themselves with cries of "We want George" and an occasional scatological scream. Mr. Nixon glared at them, too, but not with the baleful intensity that he conferred upon the veterans. The heckling was outrageous, it was bound to make friends and votes for Richard Nixon, and it was oddly effective in its impact upon him.

At the Suffolk County airport, 15 minutes by helicopter from the Nassau hall, some 3000 people had been waiting at the airport fence for three hours and more on a damp and chilly night. Mr. Nixon marched to the fence from his helicopter, spent a couple of minutes shaking hands, and then spoke for eight minutes from the ramp of his waiting plane. If such be possible, his utterances surpassed in banality his speeches at the Rockefeller reception and at Nassau. But, and this is the memorable thing, he pleased the people. They cheered his fatuities and then stood without a visible break, watching him retire into his plane with Mrs. Nixon. They continued to stand, staring at the floodlit plane, as it taxied away and leaped into the night. Their posture of frozen interest and pleasure left me thinking that Mr. Nixon is likely to get his majority and his mandate, after all.

November 4, 1972

———

In subsequent campaign appearances in Illinois, New Mexico, Rhode Island, North Carolina, and California, Mr. Nixon appeared to enjoy himself as he hadn't in New York. But throughout, the road performance was superfluous and the President seemed to know it. His staff politicians were right, I think, in saying after the election that I and other reporters never covered "the real campaign" as we should have. Mr. Nixon's "real campaign" was conducted by him at the White House, being President, and for him by the fifty-plus surrogates who blanketed the country's principal population centers.

XXXIII

Kissinger's Course

It has been Richard Nixon's war since 1969 and it will be his settlement if Henry Kissinger turns out to have been right when he said in the White House press room on October 26, in a voice charged with pride and emotion, that "peace is at hand." The official accounts of the preliminaries to the settlement predicted by Kissinger make it evident that it has been the President, not his assistant for national security affairs, who has decided what to concede and what to hold out for at every step of the current approach to a condition that may pass, at least for awhile, as peace in Indochina. But the attitudes and the world view of Henry Kissinger, meshing as they have in unique accord with the President's equivalent attitudes and view, have contributed immensely to American policy in Indochina and Vietnam during the Nixon time. Here, derived from the incomplete public and private record, is a brief review of Kissinger's contribution to the course that may in some part be called his course.

There are indications that Kissinger misread the minds of both President Thieu in Saigon and President Nixon in Washington during the critical private negotiations in Paris from October 8 through October 11. Kissinger spoke later of "the risks that were involved" when, in order to seize the promise of a settlement that

might slip away, he accepted Hanoi's revised proposals as the
working basis for "at least the outline of an agreement" and, as he
tacitly acknowledged, gave his North Vietnamese friend and an-
tagonist in secret negotiation since 1969, Le Duc Tho, reason to
believe that the draft completed on October 11 was in effect a
final agreement that the US and North Vietnamese governments
were pledged to sign before or by October 31. The risk that President Thieu would balk at the provisions for a cease-fire and a
political settlement proved to be more thoroughly justified than
Kissinger anticipated. A further impression that Kissinger also and
knowingly risked exceeding the bounds of concession that President Nixon would tolerate is supported by the Hanoi assertion
that the President in a message to Premier Pham Van Dong
"raised a number of complex points" that would have to be
cleared up while Kissinger and Tho were still working out the
agreement. It was then, I suspect, that Kissinger learned for keeps
that, as he later said in reference both to the October draft and to
the changes he soon found to be required, "we would have to
discuss anything that was negotiated (in Paris) first in Washington and then in Saigon." It appears, in short, that the difficulties
that infuriated Hanoi and frustrated the intention to sign by October 31 were not due solely to President Thieu.

Kissinger said on the 26th that his announcement of imminent
peace and his discussion of the October draft had no connection
with the November 7 presidential election. He insisted that "we
were prepared to keep this whole agreement secret until it was
consummated" and that he would not have been discussing it "had
Hanoi not revealed . . . the substance of the agreement." Kissinger's known though unstated theory that Hanoi expected Richard
Nixon to be reelected and figured it could get more concessions
before the election than it might get afterward is probably sound.
His claim that he was discussing the October agreement and explaining the delay only because and after Hanoi had revealed the
gist of the draft elides the facts. Hanoi broadcast its summary of
the October draft at 1 a.m. on the 26th, Washington time. *The
New York Times* of the 26th was out by 10 p.m. of the previous
evening with an authoritative and substantially accurate summary
of the draft. The White House story is that the *Times'* information
"came from Paris." Some of it did. Some of it came from various
Washington and Saigon sources. Some of it, including the basis for

" I BRING YOU TIDINGS OF GRAET JOL...! "

the language that gave the *Times* account its authoritative tone, came from Kissinger.

Hanoi's account of the October negotiations suggests that Kissinger might have popped up in Hanoi if all had gone as he hoped. Kissinger understood all along that Secretary of State William P. Rogers would have the ceremonial honor of signing a final agreement. A more important act is the initialing of an agreement, signifying that it has been concluded and accepted by the parties to it. The North Vietnamese account said it was agreed that "the two parties would initial the text of the agreement in Hanoi" and sign it later in Paris. There could be no more fitting reward to Henry Kissinger for his efforts over nearly four years to frame negotiable terms than the assignment to initial the result of his endeavors in Hanoi.

Hanoi claimed, and Kissinger gladly granted the truth of the claim, that the North Vietnamese proposal submitted to him on October 8 broke the long deadlock and made "at least the outline of an agreement" possible. But the key elements of the Hanoi proposal and of the agreed draft that resulted from it are foreshadowed in the proposals that President Nixon has been making since May 14, 1969, and in Kissinger's explanations and justifications of them. In June of 1969, for example, Kissinger discussed "mixed commissions" as possible alternatives to the kind of "imposed" government that Mr. Nixon has said he would never foist upon South Vietnam. The three-party Council of National Reconciliation proposed by Hanoi and agreed to by the US is such a body. Although Kissinger says now that this council would have no sovereign powers, he made a great point in 1969 of the prospect that the supervision of national elections, one of the duties assigned to the proposed council, would require a substantial transfer of power from the incumbent government to the supervisory body.

Kissinger never wavered from his assertions of belief, first made in 1969, that "sooner or later this war is going to be settled through negotiations." He thought then that productive negotiation and a settlement would come in that year or in 1970 at the latest. Proven wrong then, he has maintained ever since that it would come eventually and very suddenly, after a fierce display of force such as the Tet attacks in 1968 or the North Vietnamese offensive last spring. "I've always believed," he said in 1969, "that

Hanoi would maintain an implacable ferocity until just before they agreed to a settlement."

As any person of his sophistication must, Kissinger has understood throughout the Nixon period but has never said that the President's repeated commitment to accept and live with *any* result of national elections in South Vietnam removed the original excuse for US intervention there. The excuse was that a Communist rule of South Vietnam would endanger US security and therefore must be prevented. In 1969, soon after Mr. Nixon first made the pledge, Kissinger was asked whether he and the President were saying that the US would accept the outcome of an election won by the South Vietnamese Communists. "Yes," he answered, "we have said that and we are committed to it." When he was confronted with the general impression that any negotiated election would be rigged against the Communists, he answered that "we make no assumption that the Saigon government is foreordained to win this election and·that the Communists are bound to be a minority." But he has always evaded invitations to spell out the logical conclusion. When he was asked in 1970 whether the administration then considered the preservation of a non-Communist government in Saigon to be essential to US security, he repeated the Nixon-Kissinger cliché to the effect that "this administration will abide by the political decisions of the South Vietnamese people."

One of the intriguing indications that Kissinger's private views do not invariably conform to the official view he usually expresses is his frequent description of the Vietnam war as "a civil war." The official view since the late 1950s has been that it is not a civil war but a war between two sovereign and separate nations, the one an invader and the other invaded. When a reporter called his attention to this unorthodox contradiction in 1970, he hastily said that it was a civil war "with support from the outside." Afterward, in informal discussions, he resumed his references to "a civil war."

Kissinger's readiness to accept all the hazards and complexities of the kind of "cease-fire in place" now proposed for South Vietnam, and the fact that it amounts to fragmentary partition, dates back to 1969. He said then that some such arrangement didn't strike him as "a preposterous idea" and he has been working toward it ever since.

November 11, 1972

———

This report was the first published intimation that difficulties had
arisen between Nixon and Kissinger. For Kissinger's reaction, see
page 200.

XXXIV

More Than Ever

The signs and chants and songs said "Four More Years" and "Nixon Now, More than Ever," and in their idiotic way they provided a depressing indication of the kind of presidency that Richard Nixon is likely to give us in his second term. It predictably won't be very different from his first-term presidency unless more of the same, perhaps marked with a confident sense of rightness that was missing at the start of the Nixon tenure, is thought to constitute a meaningful difference. In the weeks between his renomination and his reelection, Mr. Nixon seemed to me to deny and defeat in advance of his victory whatever hopes there may have been that the mandate he sought and got would free him to be a more generous and compassionate, and in domestic affairs, a more creative President than he proved to be in the first term.

My own hopes along that line, and I had some, were dimmed well before the President in his few and cautious campaign utterances taught me once again (will I ever really learn?) that the qualities of generosity and compassion and true creativity that I as both citizen and journalist have wanted to discern in him simply are not there. The hopes faded when I went around the White House and its collateral offices, asking such assistants as I could get at what they expected from their President in a second term, assuming that he was reelected by a massive popular and electoral majority. Was I right or wrong, perceptive or gullible, in my supposition that a big win just might have a liberating (not necessarily a liberalizing) effect upon the President? My concern in these interviews was with Mr. Nixon's domestic attitudes and intentions rather than with his foreign policy—not in a wish to minimize his foreign successes but in a belief that it is at home, dealing with the social ills and strains of the country, that the President will be principally tested and should be principally judged in his second term. The consensus among my small but reasonably representative cross-section of White House assistants was that I was wrong and gullible. They thought it odd, and one or two thought it laughable, that I should consider it even remotely possible that the scope of a Nixon victory would affect the President's approach to domestic problems and his conception of his responsibilities and challenges at home in any material way.

At this time, soon after his renomination and before the President had begun the little conventional campaigning that he deigned to undertake, I was told again and again at the White House that Mr. Nixon believed that his primary duty as President in a second term, abroad and at home but especially at home, would be to respond to the majority will as he interpreted it and to shape and limit his initiatives accordingly. Stated in the way it was put, exluding as it did any domestic initiatives that were presupposed to offend the will and preferences of Mr. Nixon's "new majority," this seemed to me to be a notably restricted view of presidential leadership. I expected that the President would at least pretend to take a broader view of his responsibilities when and if he addressed himself to the subject for campaign purposes. In a broadcast on October 21, in radio time bought for him by his Committee for the Reelection of the President, Mr. Nixon proved his assistants to be entirely correct. He said that he was setting forth "my philosophy of government, so that the American people will know the principles which will guide me in making decisions over the next four years." The speech is a "must" document for anyone who wants to know what to expect of the reelected President, and I here accord it the attention that it should have received and didn't when it was delivered.

Mr. Nixon framed his remarks in the context of what he called the "basic human values" of "good, decent people" who should

" FOUR MORE YEARS! ... FOUR MORE YEARS! ..."

stop "letting themselves be bulldozed by anybody who presumes
to be the self-righteous moral judge of of our society." People who
resist higher taxes and "income redistribution," object to the busing of their children from neighborhood schools to other schools,
and oppose employment quotas for the benefit of the previously
disadvantaged ought not—he said—to be accused of selfishness,
bigotry and racism. On the contrary, he said, their values are
"values to be proud of—values that I shall always stand up for
when they come under attack." In this context, he then said: "The
rights of each minority must be vigorously defended—and each
minority must be protected in the opportunity to have its opinion
become accepted as the majority view. But on these basic concerns, the majority view must prevail, and leadership in a democracy is required to respond to that view." And again: ". . . you
can be sure of this: on matters affecting basic human values—on
the way Americans live their lives and bring up their children—I
am going to respect and reflect the opinion of the people themselves."

The President's espousal of these sentiments obviously won him
the votes of millions of "good, decent people" who believe with
reason that their interests have been ignored and their values have
been scorned in the name of social and racial reform. But Mr.
Nixon did not stop there. With his usual genius for oblique and
foggy indictment of those who differ with him, he suggested that a
more positive leadership than the kind he offers may come only
from arrogant types who "believe that the people just do not know
what is good for them" and who "have more faith in government
than they have in people." His mistaken and distorted view of the
alternatives open to him was expressed in these terms: "A leader
must be willing to take unpopular stands when they are necessary.
But a leader who insists on imposing on the people his own ideas
of how they should live their lives—when those ideas go directly
contrary to the values of the people themselves—does not understand the role of a leader in a democracy."

A President who supposes and in effect asserts that the only
alternative to submission to the perceived will of the majority is
the imposition of ideas that offend the majority does not understand the role of a leader in a democracy. By definition, a President who is so limited in his concept of the duties and powers of
his office is not a leader. Presidents have very little power to

impose. Trusted Presidents have immense power to persuade. Such a President might find it both necessary and feasible to tell his majority, as Mr. Nixon manifestly never will, that much of the opposition to higher taxes *is* selfish; that much of the resistance to busing for the integration of public schools *is* bigoted; and that racism *is* an element in much of the opposition to employment quotas for the benefit of black and other minorities. In the guise of respect for "the values of the people themselves," Mr. Nixon forgoes his duty and neglects his power to persuade the people who comprise his majority that the good of society may require measures that they do not welcome and have not mandated him to propose.

Much will be heard from the Nixon White House in the next few weeks, and much will be written, about the domestic programs that the reelected President intends to submit to Congress in 1973. Mr. Nixon will be preparing to test the proposition that the enormous popular majority conferred upon him by the electorate on November 7 gives him a leverage with the Democratic Congress that he has not previously had. The public will be suffocated with punditry to the effect that the leverage won't amount to much, given the election evidence that Mr. Nixon's appeal to the voters did other Republican candidates very little good and Democratic candidates for Congress very little harm. The President said over and over during the campaign that his first domestic purpose was to avoid new taxes and that he wasn't going to propose "bold new programs" that would require new or higher taxes. But neither the fiscal hold-down nor the possibility that Congress will pay less heed to his mandate than Mr. Nixon thinks it should is the factor chiefly making for a bleak and narrow second term, domestically speaking. The chief depressant is the reelected President's notion that leadership consists of determining what the majority wants and offering it nothing in the way of programs and ideas that he isn't sure it wants. Whatever else may be said for this conception of presidential responsibility, it is not a way to make the next four years "the best four years in the whole history of America."

November 18, 1972

Daddy Dick

At two meetings on the morning after the election, with senior members of the White House staff and with the Cabinet, the President said in a firm and fatherly tone that he wasn't about to make a mistake that he thought General Eisenhower made after he was reelected in 1956. Mr. Nixon thought that General Eisenhower failed to convey to the country and to the federal bureaucracy an expectation of change and a sense of movement from the first term into the second term. The President said that he intended to do what Eisenhower had failed to do and do it immediately, although he knew that doing it raised a problem. The problem was how to promise significant change in the second term without suggesting that the first term had not been all it should have been. It was rather like Benjamin Disraeli's problem when he succeeded British Prime Minister William Gladstone in 1874. A biographer had quoted Disraeli as saying that he wanted to give an impression of new vigor and purpose without disparaging the reforms instituted under Gladstone or implying that the new ministers were taking over from so many exhausted volcanoes. The President's listeners told each other afterward that he didn't mean to equate them with exhausted volcanoes, but that inference could be read into the allusion and it stung.

Mr. Nixon spoke in the same tone of kindly admonition at both

WHITE HOUSE REORGANIZATION

1972, The Register
and Tribune Syndicate
© THE LOS ANGELES TIMES, 1972
CONRAD

meetings when he got down to serious business. He said at the
staff meeting that he knew that some people didn't want to leave
the administration and some did. Some wanted to leave the government; some wanted to stay, but in new jobs at the White House
or in the departments and agencies; some wanted to stay where
they were. He wanted to know from them what they wanted, so
that there would be an understanding between him and them of
what everybody wanted. In the interest of orderly procedure and
early decision, so that everybody would soon know where everybody stood, he wanted to have their written resignations and the
resignations of all of the subordinate assistants who worked under
them in hand within two days, no later than November 10, along
with a written indication of each individual's preferences. He
didn't intend to discuss individual preferences and his own wishes
and intentions at this time, but everybody should understand that
their preferences would be respected and followed to the extent
possible. He was serious about reorganizing and reducing the
bureaucracy at the White House and throughout the federal government, for greater efficiency and better work by fewer people,
but there should be no cause for worry about that. It could and
would be accomplished largely by attrition and reassignment. At
the Cabinet meeting, he promised each department head a private
talk about his preferences and prospects. All of them were instructed to deliver their resignations and the resignations of the
presidential appointees working under them to the White House
by the 10th. They also were told to obtain and hold for action as
directed the resignations of the hundreds of non-presidential appointees in key departmental jobs and submit to the White House
staff written recommendations for any reorganization of their departments and bureaus that they considered desirable and practi-
cable. It was all very restrained, very gentlemanly and—as some
of the participants realized later—very cold.

Second thoughts about the exercise began with the realization
that the President really didn't have to say anything he said at the
meetings. Pesidential appointees, from department heads down,
customarily and always submit resignations toward the end of a
term. Non-presidential appointees in the "Schedule C" and "non-
career executive" jobs that Mr. Nixon was talking about know

that they serve at the pleasure of their superiors, the President included, and can be transferred at will or fired on 30 days' notice. White House staff resignations are also customary and automatic, and in any case many of them had been called for and submitted before the election. The several White House assistants who had already indicated their intention to leave the administration at the end of the first term or early in the second term would now be subject to the suspicion that they had been invited out, with possible damage to their reputations and value in the private job market. One of the immediate results was a good deal of confusion in the departments. There are some 600 presidential appointees of the kind Mr. Nixon had in mind, 600 non-career executive appointees, and 1200 "Schedule C" appointees in federal service. Fred Malek, the President's chief personnel recruiter and hatchet man, had to distribute a confidential memo to the department heads, telling them that the President didn't intend them to demand the resignations of all of the 1800 "Schedule C" and non-career appointees. The department heads were to use their judgment, asking only for resignations from jobs that were deemed to rate presidential notice and possible replacement, and the holders of those jobs were to be assured that relatively few of them would be fired.

So, why did the President do it? He did it for public effect, and he soon got more of the effect than he wanted. Press Secretary Ronald Ziegler, summarizing the gist of the President's remarks for the media soon after the post-election meetings, did his best to put the emphasis on "restructuring" rather than upon the fate of individuals at the White House and elsewhere. But he and the President, who had told him what to say and why it was to be said, miscalculated on two counts. White House reporters, hungry for meaty news after a thin and dreary presidential reelection campaign, jumped at Ziegler's initial announcement like starved dogs at a beef haunch. The result was some exaggerated speculation that 2000 or more executive firings and a wholesale shakeup of the bureaucracy were in prospect. At the White House and in the departments, the President's remarks as relayed by the officials who heard them had generally been received with patient and rather cynical good humor. The publicity had an unsettling effect, however, raising alarm and confusion where the President wanted comprehension, and causing a good many of his servitors at the White House and elsewhere to reflect that Mr. Nixon is all too capable of sacrificing them, his soft words notwithstanding, to his own desires and interests.

The other miscalculation was that anybody with any sense and sophistication could be long impressed by the trumpeted reorganization and bureaucratic reform. However serious the President may be in his ambition to improve the processes of government and the services delivered by government, and he must be believed when he says he is altogether serious about it, the resort to it to create the impression of significant change and movement that he sought was bound to be recognized for what it is, a confession of extreme programmatic poverty. Bureaucratic restructuring and reorganization, more efficient work from fewer people, "reform" in the sense of diffusing federal responsibility among state and local governments, were familiar and tired Nixon themes by the time the President finished the second year of his first term. Granting that there may be nothing wrong with them except age, there was something pathetic in the spectacle of a President, just endowed with the first national majority and mandate he had ever won, relying upon them to foster confidence that his second term is going to be exciting and productive.

The President said in an interview that he expects his second term to be exciting and productive "on the domestic front." He gave the interview to Garnett Horner of *The Washington Star-News* on the Sunday before the election, with the proviso that it appear after the election. In it are the most revealing words that Richard Nixon has ever spoken. Explaining why his next version of welfare reform is going to put more emphasis upon work requirements than on welfare support, the President said: "The average American is just like a child in the family. You give him some responsibility and he is going to amount to something. He is going to do something. If, on the other hand, you make him completely dependent and pamper him and cater to him too much, you are going to make him soft, spoiled, and eventually a very weak individual."

Yes, Daddy.

November 25, 1972

XXXVI

Camping Out

The charade with which the President chose to begin the transition to his second term continued into Thanksgiving week. After four days in almost complete seclusion at his Florida home on Key Biscayne, he flew back to Washington for one night at the White House and then withdrew into even more complete isolation, so far as the press and public were concerned, for a stay of unprecedented length at Camp David, the retreat maintained for Presidents since Franklin Roosevelt's day in the Maryland mountains an hour's ride by car and thirty-five minutes by helicopter from Washington.

"Charade" has to be qualified. It was all for public effect: the initial forecasts of staff and departmental reorganization, at the White House and throughout the federal government; the daily procession of Cabinet members, agency heads and favored White House assistants to Camp David for an hour or so of conversation with the President; Press Secretary Ronald Ziegler's cautions to reporters, in briefings conducted in a huge trailer installed for the purpose at the guarded entrance to Camp David, that they mustn't assume from his and the President's talk of shaking up the federal establishment that hundreds of executive heads are about to roll. As I have written, it was the only way the President could think of—and a rather feeble way—to create an impression that his second term is going to be, on the domestic front, much more than a mere and sterile extension of the first term. Because the President had ruled out most of the possibilities for positive advance and innovation in domestic policy, unless the demolition and contraction of present programs can be called advance and innovation, a show of determination to shrink and tighten up the administrative structure was all he had to offer. In Mr. Nixon's view, however, that is a great deal. It's serious business, to be taken as seriously by the public and by the federal bureaucracy as he takes it. He's had this thing about staffing and structure ever since he became President, and never mind that in dramatizing his intention to begin the process of administrative reduction and reform with his own structure at the White House he invites a wonder as to how and why he let it get to be the biggest in presidential history.

The transition performance provided some interesting glimpses of Richard Nixon at work on his people. Camp David is a cluster of quasi-rustic cottages buried in the woods, an informal place where you might expect a President to slip into casual clothing for his conversations with his appointees. Not this President. In the cottage that he has had transformed from living into office quarters, he greeted his callers in the same business suits that he wears at the White House. The talk at the meetings was at once easy and grave, tinged in some cases by the strain of people telling the President everything he wanted to know about their wishes and learning little or nothing from him about his intentions. He had said in advance of the visits that he was giving himself until December 15 to announce his personnel decisions, and in most instances his callers were still awaiting December 15 when they left him at Camp David.

Defense Secretary Melvin Laird, who months ago announced his intention to resign at the end of the first term, told an associate after his session that he didn't know whom the President had in mind to succeed him and what, if any, replacements Mr. Nixon planned to make at lower reaches of the department. Secretary of State William P. Rogers, the President's oldest and closest friend in the administration, appeared to his subordinates to be in somewhat better shape after his Camp David conversation. He spoke with seeming assurance of future plans for the department and his own activities as Secretary, including a probable visit to Europe with the President next February. Although Secretary Rogers was saying until a year ago that one term would be enough for him, he has been indicating since then that he'd like to remain well into the second term. His demeanor just before and after he met with the President at Camp David suggested that the rumors of his being replaced by John B. Connally, the Texas Nixocrat and former Secretary of the Treasury, in preparation for a horrendous shakeout of the State Department and Foreign Service bureaucracies, are groundless nonsense. But the Secretary's associates won't know for sure that he knows for sure until the President announces his new Cabinet lineup.

The assumption at the State Department, not questioned by Rogers, is that Henry Kissinger will stay on as the President's assistant for national security affairs. Kissinger has been saying since early 1972 that he will know when it's time to go and that he intends to do so before the second term is far along. If the President has read and thoroughly absorbed an incredibly vainglorious and imperious interview that Kissinger gave a lady journalist from Italy on November 4, replete with suggestions that he alone is responsible for the approach to a settlement in Vietnam and accommodation with Communist China, among other Nixon achievements in foreign policy, the departure could occur sooner than Kissinger contemplates. Secretive by habit and preoccupied as he has been with making his announcement that "peace is at hand" in Vietnam come true, Kissinger has said nothing about his plans to his numerous National Security Council staff. The Kissinger staff has been immune from the general call at the White House for resignations that the President can ignore or accept as he pleases. At an unannounced meeting on November 13, one of the few that Kissinger has ever taken the trouble and time to have with his entire staff, the subject of resignations and reorganization didn't come up. This, contrary to the claim that everybody on the Nixon staff is on the White House payroll, is partly because key members of the NSC staff are seconded to it from the career Foreign Service and are on the State Department payroll.

One of the few resignations demanded with the declared intention of accepting it was that of the Rev. Theodore M. Hesburgh, chairman of the US Commission on Civil Rights and the only remaining one of the five members originally appointed to the commission in 1957 by Mr. Nixon's late patron, President Eisenhower. In a "Dear Ted" letter in 1969, Mr. Nixon publicly thanked Father Hesburgh, the president of Notre Dame University, for his stand against campus disorder. Since then, Father Hesburgh and the commission have been outspoken in their criticism of the Nixon civil rights performance and, most recently, in their denunciation of the President's inflammatory use and distortion of the school busing issue. Mr. Nixon lacked the grace to tell Father Hesburgh that his resignation was wanted, or even to have a responsible assistant do it. While the commission was meeting in Washington on November 13, a secretary to Fred Malek, the President's chief recruiter, telephoned the demand to John Buggs, the commission's staff director, who passed it to the chairman. Father Hesburgh replied as follows on November 16: "Dear Mr. Nixon: In compliance with your request, transmitted by Mr. Frederic Malek of the White House staff, I hereby submit my resignation as chairman and member of the United States Commission on Civil Rights. Best regards. Cordially yours . . ." Father Hesburgh and Stephen Horn, the commission vice chairman, dined on the 13th with Leonard Garment, the President's special consultant on minority problems and sensibilities. It is said to have been a pleasant dinner, unmarred by mention of the crude and cowardly way in which this particular bit of reform was accomplished.

Len Garment is one of several White House assistants who intended to quit but are staying on, after exposure to Mr. Nixon's persuasive talk that he wants and needs them. Another may be Harry Dent, the White House specialist in southern politics, who announced his decision to resign last July and was all set to go back to Columbia, SC, when the President sweet-talked him at Camp David. At this writing, Dent is trying to brace himself to tell the President that he still intends to quit. Patrick Buchanan, a senior speech writer who hoped to replace Frank Shakespeare, the departing director of the US Information Agency, was told he couldn't do that but would have new and broader responsibilities at the White House. So he's staying, and glad to do it. The White House is a hard place to leave and the President knows it.

December 2, 1972

———

Henry Dent braced himself and quit. I underestimated the number of changes intended by the President, but not, I think, the element of cruel and phoney showmanship involved.

XXXVII

Kicking Sand

In the fourth week of what Press Secretary Ronald Ziegler called the President's endeavor "to treat the beginning of the second term as a completely fresh start for this administration," a White House assistant offered comfort of a sort to a federal bureau chief who wanted to know whether he will have a job when Mr. Nixon gets through moving department heads and lesser officials from place to place and bringing in a few new appointees. By way of reminding the bureau chief that he had company in misery, the assistant said, "This is a period when a lot of people are standing around, kicking sand." William Safire, a Nixon writer who earned large sums in the public relations business and will be in a position to earn larger sums when and if he leaves the White House staff, dealt in what he considered to be a definitive way with the suspicion that there is more atmosphere than substance in the successive announcements of personnel changes and non-changes at White House, Cabinet and lower administration levels. "Atmosphere," Safire said, "*is* substance."

The President, who is known to be capable of spontaneous laughter, must have got a laugh out of his success in compelling the media to serve his purposes by reporting as big news the non-news that he had decided, after grave deliberation, to keep several of his Cabinet members and department heads where they already were. Secretaries William P. Rogers at State, George P. Shultz at Treasury, Rogers C. B. Morton at Interior, Earl Butz at Agriculture, and Richard Kleindienst at Justice are staying put, at least for now, and the justifiable reaction in each case would be but hasn't been—so what? The central meaning, not altered in any important respect by the changes that also have been and are to be announced, is that the second Nixon term isn't going to be very different in either cast or posture from the first Nixon term. The governing tone and policies of the Nixon administration are set at the White House, not in the departments and agencies. The signal that there isn't going to be meaningful change at the White House was loud and clear a month after the President's reelection. It was the announcement that John D. Ehrlichman, the assistant for domestic affairs; H. R. Haldeman, the administrative chief; Peter Flanigan, who doubles as emissary to big business and director of the Council on International Economic Policy, and most of the other principal assistants are remaining in essentially unchanged roles. Henry Kissinger is a special case and I'll be getting to his situation and prospects later in this report.

A new role assigned to George Shultz is a matter of the mechanics of power and decision, not of change in presidential purpose and policy. Shultz is to be both Treasury secretary and an assistant to the President at the head of a new Council on Economic Policy. In his words, he and the council are "to provide an identified, explicitly identified, group and person responsible to the President for the overall relating of different aspects of economic policy." The "overall relating" of domestic and foreign economic policy is said to be the principal purpose, and there is no intention to derogate the aim when the President's addiction to councils is noted. Various members of the Council on Economic Policy are also members of the Domestic Council, the Cost of Living Council, and Peter Flanigan's Council on International Economic Policy. Herbert Stein, who stays as chairman of the statutory Council of Economic Advisers, is a member of all of them. When Shultz was asked whether his added responsibilities and eminence might bring him into conflict with the President on major economic policy questions, he delivered a memorable sermonette on the realities of presidential counsel and decision, Nixon style. Shultz said: "No. It doesn't work that way at all. . . . You never get yourself in a position where people proceed along on something that important and fundamental, as though the President is not there, and then confront him with something that is not in keeping with his thinking. That is just not the way the policy process works or certainly not the way I would want to have it work." This passage is recommended to journalists and others who suspect that serious disputes between the President and his advisers are hidden. They don't occur at the Nixon White House.

Proximity to Presidents is important in all administrations and especially important in this one, Mr. Nixon being a President who prefers to do business in person with the smallest feasible number of people. Shultz had the fact in mind when he welcomed assurance that he and a small staff will have offices in the West Wing, where the President works when he can't arrange to work somewhere else. An assistant who also understands the value of proximity is Special Counsel Charles Colson. His office in the Executive Office Building, a few steps across West Executive Avenue from the White House and the West Wing, adjoins an office the President took for himself soon after he was inaugurated in 1969 and frequently uses. Colson has a unique way of calling the attention of visitors to his location. When voices are raised, he shushes offenders with the caution that they mustn't risk disturbing the President next door. Colson, a lawyer who has proven himself to be a skillful and ruthless political tactician in the President's service, has probably seen more of Mr. Nixon in recent months than any domestic assistant excepting Haldeman and Ehrlichman. His reputation as the President's dirty-tricks man, not to mention his vague and undocumented association in news accounts with the Watergate bugging and campaign sabotage scandals, has not impaired the frequency and intimacy of his association with Mr. Nixon. But it has been a largely hidden intimacy, never willingly publicized, and some of Colson's White House colleagues connect this fact with the announcement that he is leaving the staff in early 1973. The impression of these colleagues has been that Colson would be glad to continue to forgo the hundreds of thousands of dollars in annual income that he can earn as a Washington lawyer-lobbyist and stay on at the top staff salary of $42,500 a year, if he were accorded the formal recognition and status that Haldeman,

Ehrlichman and a few Counsellors with Cabinet rank have enjoyed. In announcing Colson's imminent departure, Press Secretary Ziegler lavished upon him expressions of the President's esteem and gratitude with a fervor not manifested toward any other departing official. While doing so on the President's orders, Ziegler presumably has been aware of Colson's recommendation that the press secretary's functions and staff be merged with those of Herbert Klein, the Director of Communications. Colson has also recommended that his protegé and Klein's deputy, Ken W. Clawson, be placed in charge of the merged operation when and if Klein leaves the White House. For several reasons, including the President's fondness for Ziegler and Ziegler's cool relationship with Clawson, this probably won't happen.

Now we get to Henry Kissinger. In my opinion, stated here in order to put what follows in the proper perspective, Henry Kissinger is the most talented and valuable assistant in the President's service. I as a citizen am extremely glad that he's been at the White House and I'll be extremely sorry when he leaves, which I expect him to do in the fairly near future. Like several other Nixon assistants who may be expected to depart before the second term is far along, Kissinger conveys an impression that whether and when he leaves is for him to decide, the President having decided and told the assistants in question that he wants them to stay as long as they are willing to. Kissinger has recently told me and other reporters that "I will make my final decision about my future relationship after this Vietnam thing is wound up and I have a chance to go away for a few weeks and think."

Kissinger toyed in early 1972 with the thought that he might succeed Secretary of State Rogers and had the sense to be brought up short by two reflections. One of them was that he with his arbitrary ways of action and management (or non-management), and the State Department with its sedate attitudes and procedures, simply could not tolerate each other for very long. The other reflection was that he at the State Department and a successor at the White House with anything approaching his stature and brilliance, plus the aforementioned ways of working, could not coexist and function together as a President would have to require them to function. A corollary of this last thought, and one that in my guess has troubled Kissinger, is the probability that the National Security Council structure that he has developed for the President cannot survive his departure. He used to talk with passion of his hope that it would be a lasting contribution to the institution of the presidency. He doesn't talk that way now, to my limited knowledge, and I think it's because he realizes—without benefit or compulsion of his abundant vanity—that the present NSC structure is too closely identified with and bound up with him to be even remotely the same after he leaves it.

A revealing brush with Kissinger resulted from my suggestion in *The New Republic* that in his October negotiations with Le Duc Tho, the ones that led to the aborted agreement of October 11, he went beyond the limits of concession to the North Vietnamese that President Nixon was prepared to allow. Other publications made the same point and the Thieu propagandists in Saigon made a lot of it. The brush occurred when I queried Kissinger about a sequence of events that I still find odd and puzzling. During the President's first post-election visit to Florida, when Nixon and Kissinger were lodged for three days within a few minutes' drive of each other, they never met in person and talked only by telephone. Later, on a Saturday when the President flew to Washington from his mountain haven at Camp David with the announced purpose of consulting with Kissinger, they again talked only by telephone although they were within yelling distance of each other at the White House. When he was asked what the telephoning meant, Kissinger answered: "Look, you have had a theory that I thought has been really extraordinarily mischievous, that there's been some sort of trouble between the President and me and that I overstepped my instructions and all that sort of baloney. Well, I assure you that it is totally, 100 percent wrong and that whoever told you this, you should never put any credence into again." I told him that nobody planted the notion with me; it was my reading of his and Hanoi's accounts of the October negotiations. When he was asked again about "the telephone thing," he answered: "It's a fact, but it doesn't mean what you think it means. I assure you that it has nothing to do with him and me or any strain between him and me."

During the current Kissinger-Tho negotiations in Paris, Press Secretary Ziegler has said repeatedly and with unprecedented emphasis that Kissinger is acting on the President's instructions and has been getting constant instructions from the President. That's believable, too. As I wrote in the piece that disturbed Kissinger, it's been Richard Nixon's war since 1969 and it will be his settlement if there is one.

December 16, 1972

XXXVIII

Bombs Away

When the President undertook on Monday, December 18, to bomb the North Vietnamese back into the Paris negotiations that he had terminated on the 13th, he had gone 32 days without saying a word in public about the Vietnam war and his hopes of ending it with "a peace that will last." When he had a spokesman announce on December 30 that the negotiations were to be resumed and that the bombing of Hanoi, Haiphong and other places in the heartland of North Vietnam had been halted, he still had said nothing in person and in public about the war, the bombardment, the worldwide revulsion that the bombardment caused, its heavy cost in men and planes, and the elusive settlement. While hundreds of American B-52s and other planes were dropping ruin and death on North Vietnam, and during the first four days after the worst of the bombardment was suspended, the President appeared only twice in public, apart from fleeting passage through Washington, Florida and Kansas City airports. He dined with Mrs. Nixon and his friend C. G. Rebozo at a hotel near his Florida home, and he did brief homage to Harry Truman at his bier and home in Independence. In this same period, he never once permitted his White House spokesmen to say that he had ordered the expanded and intensified bombing of North Vietnam or even that he had authorized the short pauses over the Christmas and New Year holidays that in fact occurred. At the White House, at Camp David in the Maryland mountains, at his home on Key Biscayne, and again at Camp David and the White House for a lonely New Year weekend, the President kept himself in almost total silence and seclusion. His daughters and their husbands were in Europe. Mrs. Nixon flew on New Year's Eve morning to the Rose Bowl ceremonies in Pasadena. When a reporter asked Deputy Press Secretary Gerald Warren whether Mr. Nixon was really and wholly alone at the White House on New Year's Eve night, Warren answered, "Well, Manolo was here." Manolo Sanchez, the President's valet and friend, is a merry fellow, utterly devoted to Mr. Nixon. For a President troubled and laden as this President must have been—could the blood and tears and wreck of North Vietnam have been altogether curtained from him?—Manolo Sanchez may have been the company he needed and was the only company he allowed himself on the night that ushered in the first year of his second term.

Aside from the mentioned exceptions and two others (he was photographed on New Year's Day with a winning football coach and recorded a tribute the next day to Roberto Clemente, a Puerto Rican baseball player for the Pittsburgh Pirates who was killed in a plane crash), the President chose during the period in review to portray himself to the country and the world solely through his press spokesmen, Ronald Ziegler and Gerald Warren. They dealt with many matters other than Vietnam. But they could not get away from Vietnam. The terror unleashed there, the terror that they were instructed not to acknowledge as terror or to attribute to the President, dominated the news and the questions addressed to them. Forty-eight hours before Ziegler, the chief spokesman, began to field the questions brought on by the new bombing, Henry Kissinger announced that his October, November and December meetings in Paris with Hanoi's principal negotiator, Le Duc Tho, had failed to produce an agreement that "the President considers just and fair." The contrast between this confession and Kissinger's earlier assurance that peace was at hand was beginning to shock and numb the country when, at the White House on the 18th, Ziegler set the tone of the weird time that followed.

Ziegler, a bland and personable young man who is a master at purveying evasive claptrap when the President prescribes evasive

claptrap, was asked why bombing had been ordered on a scale
never before ordered in Vietnam and Indochina. For starters, he
refused to say that bombing on any scale had been ordered. The
fact that it had been was not announced, then or later, at either
the White House or the Pentagon. Defense Secretary Melvin Laird
and his Pentagon spokesmen merely confirmed reports from Saigon
that renewed mining of Haiphong harbor and bombing throughout
North Vietnam, in areas where no bombing had occurred since
October, had been authorized. Avoiding such ugly words as bombs
and bombing, Ziegler referred only to "actions which the Secretary
of Defense and the Defense Department have mentioned this
morning." He nearly slipped up when he was asked, "Why did the
President order a resumption of the full-scale air activities over
North Vietnam?" and didn't dispute the way the query was stated.
When he was asked whether he meant to acknowledge that "we
have resumed full-scale air activity against the North," he said
that "I am not characterizing the activity at all. I am referring to
my statement." His statement, part of a previous answer, was that
"The actions . . . are designed to cope with another enemy buildup
and to prevent yet another round of offensive actions by the enemy
in the southern part of Vietnam." It also included assertions,
echoing Henry Kissinger on the 16th, that "we stand ready to
negotiate in a serious and constructive manner, to achieve the right
kind of settlement," and that the right kind of settlement could be
achieved whenever "the North Vietnamese make the decision to
proceed in a constructive way and in the spirit of good will."

Ziegler's, meaning the President's, major and recurring theme
on the 18th and at four subsequent press briefings in Washington
and Florida was that "the actions" in North Vietnam reflected and
expressed the policy stated by the President in a televised speech
on May 8. This was the speech in which the President announced
the mining of North Vietnamese harbors and intensified bombing
in order to cut off Soviet and Communist Chinese supplies to North
Vietnam. It was his response and counter to the invasion of South
Vietnam which North Vietnam launched across the Demilitarized
Zone on March 31. The May speech was relevant to the December
situation and bombing only in the sense that the President had
said that "these actions . . . will cease" when the North Vietnamese
agree to return "all American prisoners of war" and to accept "an
internationally supervised ceasefire throughout Indochina." Was

he saying in December, through Ziegler, that the current and much more savage "actions" would cease only when the North Vietnamese signaled their readiness at least to discuss terms for a settlement that had been broadened well beyond the two conditions set forth in May? Indeed he was, without admitting that this was what he was saying. It was deemed more prudent, more acceptable to what remained of the popular conscience, to prate about frustrating a menacing and abnormal North Vietnamese military buildup. Perhaps because Washington and Saigon reporters with access to American intelligence officials found no evidence of such a buildup, the President (through Ziegler) modified the claim with talk of "a contingent buildup" and edged close to saying that the purpose of the bombing was to bludgeon the North Vietnamese into a suitably pliant mood and back to the conference table that they kept offering to return to if the President stopped the bombing. Thus Ziegler in Florida, December 21, referring to a reduction of the bombing in October: "The steps that we took between May 8 and now [sic] were steps that were taken because negotiations were proceeding in a constructive way. My announcement the other day [December 18], in which I told you that the May 8 policy is in effect because the North Vietnamese were not proceeding in their negotiations in a constructive way, I think was quite clear." Rightly interpreted, it was.

The Nixons dined at their Key Biscayne home with "Bebe" Rebozo on Christmas Eve and Christmas night. It was officially announced that Mr. and Mrs. Nixon "exchanged Christmas presents" on Christmas morning. It was not announced, but came out, that the President sold two Key Biscayne lots at a profit of around $100,000. After the return to Washington, the tributary flight to the Truman home, and the President's retirement into New Year silence, it fell to Jerry Warren (Ziegler being on holiday in California) to announce that the bombing of Hanoi and Haiphong had been discontinued "as soon at it was clear that serious negotiations could be resumed."

January 6 and 13, 1973

———

Did the December bombing accomplish its purpose and force the North Vietnamese to conclude the "agreement to end the war and bring peace with honor in Vietnam and in Southeast Asia" that the President announced on January 23, 1973? Henry Kissinger was asked as much on January 24 and answered: "I can only say that we resumed the negotiations on January 8 and the breakthrough occurred on January 9 and I will let those facts speak for themselves."

XXXIX

These Four Years

In a note sent to several White House assistants on December 12, I said I was preparing a review of Mr. Nixon's first four years in the presidency and continued: "I wonder if you'd be willing to think back over your time at the White House and recall for my use two or three highlights of the experience—whether involving the President, yourself alone or with others, anything serious or trivial that you especially remember." The same request was made in person to other assistants. Because Henry Kissinger was in Paris at the time, and also because Kissinger's assistants on the National Security Council staff understand that he alone is permitted to associate and communicate in any meaningful way with reporters, the inquiry was confined to people on the President's domestic staff. Not at all to my surprise, the request was ignored by John D. Ehrlichman, the assistant for domestic affairs; H. R. Haldeman, the administrative chief; and Peter Flanigan, who looks after international economic matters and the President's relations with business moguls. Special Counsel Charles Colson responded after a fashion, in a way that I thought irrelevant to my request but nonetheless understandable, considering my tendency to refer to him as the President's dirty-tricks man and to neglect his numerous other services, which Mr. Nixon has had a spokesman say he greatly values. Colson had his secretary say by telephone, with what sounded like a couple of apologetic giggles: "He said, since you're thoroughly convinced that he's an s.o.b., it would take an undue amount of time to try to convince you otherwise and it probably wouldn't accomplish anything." Maybe and maybe not. But the response left me wondering, as I've been wondering these four years, at the obtuseness of some of the smartest people in the President's employ. They are too dumb, or perhaps too locked in the paranoia that grips the Nixon White House, to grasp the fact that reporters as a species, this reporter included, are suckers for officials who at least go through the motions of confiding in them now and then and providing a version, however weighted it may be, of what goes on.

Three points have to be made before getting to some of the slightly more productive responses that I did receive. The first point is that the quoted assistants were talking about a President who would soon be resuming the unrestricted bombing of North Vietnam in order to obtain a settlement of the war that he (in Henry Kissinger's words) "considers just and fair" and that (in his own words) he can accept "without staining the honor of the United States." The second point is that the responses typify the reluctance of Mr. Nixon's assistants to say or tell anything about him that comes anywhere near disclosing, in any but the blandest generalities and the most innocuous anecdotes, the private man behind the public façade.

The third point is that the assistants had been asked to recall highlights of their parts in a term that has been marked by a good deal of solid accomplishment, abroad and at home. The Nixon version of the record is set forth in a White House paper that runs to 43 single-spaced folio pages and 20,000 words. It is understated and factual on the whole, larded with less exaggeration and evasion of unpleasant qualifying circumstances than is to be expected in such a document. It is true, for instance, that the turmoils that racked the country when Mr. Nixon took office have been quieted (though one may doubt that the quietude really signifies the healing that the President promised in his 1969 inaugural address). The economy has been stabilized and set on an upward trend and Mr. Nixon's wage-price controls, which he proposes to extend, have done more violence to his own past principles of unfettered enterprise than they have to national and individual well-being.

Critics who marvel at the omission of any reference to the cumulative budget deficit of around $100 billion during the first Nixon years must acknowledge that Mr. Nixon never promised in 1968 to bring the budget into literal balance and that his deficits have had the sought effect of controlled stimulus.

In view of Mr. Nixon's recent expressions of scorn for the idea that the nation's inward ills can be cured by "throwing dollars at the problems," the scores of boasts that this President is spending more money on education, minority needs, protection of the environment, housing, health, urban recovery, rural development, the arts and humanities and what-have-you than any President before him has spent invite sardonic notice. But the claim of effort and of some success in many domestic problem areas is justified. So, it at least may be hoped, is the claim in the discussion of foreign policy that the Cold War has been "diminished if not ended by the President's successful Summit trips" to Peking and Moscow and the agreements that resulted. This cannot be said of the confident references to a "prospective agreement" to end the Vietnam war and a statement that "the US role" in a "Vietnam peace settlement" has been "virtually completed." In this season of frustration and expanded American attack, they serve only to document the case that Mr. Nixon and his negotiator and counsellor, Henry Kissinger, didn't know where they stood and what they were doing in this matter when the White House record of "change that works" was put together in early December.

Now for the promised responses and their sparse indications of what some of the President's assistants remember from the four years and, in some instances, from association with Mr. Nixon before he won the presidency.

Henry Cashen, 33, is a lawyer and a deputy assistant to the President. Cashen works with Charles Colson and has been involved with him in creating a remarkably complete system of contact with trade associations, ethnic groups, organized labor, the Catholic hierarchy and many other sources of prospective and actual support for the President and his policies. Of course without describing the process in intimate detail, Cashen remembers the skill with which the President took charge of the 1972 reelection effort about six months before election day and directed it while seeming to remain in a state of lofty detachment. The President's appeal to usually Democratic Catholic voters with his public stand against abortion, his promises of aid to parochial schools, and his courtesies to church dignitaries is recalled with special admiration. "The way he cracked that Catholic vote," Cashen says, "is unbelievable." Cashen, then three years out of law school, traveled with Nixon as a volunteer advance man during the 1966 congressional campaign. He remembers how the sometime Vice President, then widely marked off as a loser and not sure he wasn't, took heart from the crowds he drew at airport rallies and a year later, in 1967, showed with rising ebullience and vigor his feeling that "he was really back in the ball game." He remembers being with Colson, John Ehrlichman, George Shultz (now Treasury Secretary) and former Postmaster General Winton Blount when they reported to Nixon with some trepidation that the only way to deal with a strike of postal workers was to send the army into the New York City post office, and hearing the President say with wry amusement that he'd come to that conclusion without their help. There are "the little things" that Cashen and other assistants recount with suffocating regularity and genuine conviction, such as the President's courtesies to wives and visiting parents and his flair for pleasing them with the recollection of small details about them. It's one of the qualities that causes Cashen to say, "He's a very warm person and a very tough guy" and "There's nothing I wouldn't do for Richard Nixon."

Raymond K. Price, Jr., a reformed journalist who heads the White House writing staff, remembers a long memorandum that the President dictated after he visited a group of young antiwar protesters at the Lincoln Memorial in the dawn hours of a morning in May 1970, after he'd ordered the invasion of Cambodia. The memorandum recorded the frustration and disappointment the President felt when he read and heard news accounts of the episode. The youngsters had said, and the media had reported with relish, that all he could talk about was football and surfing and such. The President thought he'd been misunderstood and misinterpreted: he said in his memo that he was just trying to reach his hearers with the sports talk and then to get across to them some sense of his anguish and of his belief, however unlikely it might seem to them, that history would prove him to have been right. Ray Price also remembers his bitterness—his word—over what he calls "the despicable way McGovern handled the war issue at the end." His reference is to Senator McGovern's doubts, now proven to have been correct, that the draft Vietnam agreement disclosed by Hanoi and confirmed by Henry Kissinger in late October was a durable agreement that would bring the promised peace. "He had been briefed, he had seen the agreement, and he knew it was not a fraud," Price says of McGovern. Price is under the impression, widespread at the White House, that an authentic text of the October draft had been passed to McGovern through former Assistant Secretary of Defense Paul Warnke, who was getting White House briefings for the senator's benefit. Warnke says that he was briefed in some detail on October 28 but was neither shown nor given a text and thus never had one to give McGovern. It's a minor point, academic now, but indicative of the feeling in the President's vicinity that his opponent and not Richard Nixon was the tricky and devious candidate in 1972.

Edward L. Morgan, a deputy assistant to the President and deputy director of the Domestic Council under John Ehrlichman, never once mentioned a personal contact with the President during 40 minutes of shared remembrance. The closest he came to it was his recollection of being taken along on a visit to a navy carrier and of occasional invitations to state dinners. "I don't want to make it sound corny," Morgan says, recalling the carrier trip, "but the memorable part of it is, the President cares enough to take the little guys along." One of Morgan's many domestic tasks was to work on the original version, now in limbo, of the President's welfare reform program. He remembers the thrill he got when he and Richard Nathan, an expert on the subject and a former assistant, were with Governor Nelson Rockefeller in New York City and received a telephone call from John Ehrlichman in Bucharest. Ehrlichman, there with the President at the end of a round-the-world journey in 1969, said Mr. Nixon needed to know what Rockefeller thought of the welfare draft before approving it. Morgan told Ehrlichman that the governor thought well of it and the episode looms high in his memory of "the first really big one I was on." Morgan is to be an assistant secretary of the treasury and he looks forward with obvious pleasure to being "part of the President's team in the departments."

Lee Huebner, a writer on Ray Price's staff, remembers submitting the draft of a speech to the President last April, in the living room of his lodge at Camp David in the Maryland mountains near Washington. It was night time and the President was sitting alone in the dark, lights off, thinking. Huebner got back his draft the next morning with a scrawl across the top of the first page: "Lee— okay—good job—RN—4:30 a.m." He surmised later that the President must have been pondering the recent North Vietnamese attack on northern South Vietnam and his decision, then in the making and soon to be announced, to intensify the bombardment of North Vietnam and mine its harbors. Mr. Nixon said on May 8 that he had to do it in order to end the war. Near the close of the first four years, he is doing it again in order to end the war.

December 23 and 30, 1972

INDEX